EDEXCEL INTERNATIONAL GCSE

HISTORY
RUSSIA AND THE SOVIET UNION, 1905–24
Student Book

Rob Bircher

Series Editor: Nigel Kelly

Published by Pearson Education Limited, 80 Strand, London, WC2R 0RL.

www.pearsonglobalschools.com

Copies of official specifications for all Pearson qualifications may be found on the website: https://qualifications.pearson.com

Text © Pearson Education Limited 2017
Edited by Sze Kiu Yeung and Juliet Gardner
Designed by Cobalt id and Pearson Education Limited
Typeset and illustrated by Phoenix Photosetting Ltd
Original illustrations © Pearson Education Limited 2017
Cover design by Pearson Education Limited
Picture research by Andreas Schindler
Cover photo/illustration Mary Evans Picture Library
Inside front cover Shutterstock.com: Dmitry Lobanov

The rights of Rob Bircher to be identified as author of this work have been asserted by him in accordance with the Copyright, Designs and Patents Act 1988.

First published 2017

19 18
10 9 8 7 6 5 4 3

British Library Cataloguing in Publication Data
A catalogue record for this book is available from the British Library

ISBN 978 0 4351 8543 5

Printed in Slovakia by Neografia

Acknowledgements
The author and publisher would like to thank the following individuals and organisations for permission to reproduce their photographs:
(Key: b-bottom; c-centre; l-left; r-right; t-top)

Alamy Stock Photo: Chronicle 11br, 77c, Everett Collection Historical 44, Granger Historical Picture Archive / © DACS 60br, Heritage Image Partnership Ltd 82br, INTERFOTO 6tr, 81tr, John Frost Newspapers 37br, Photo 12 4tr, SPUTNIK 45tr, 49br, 96br
Bridgeman Art Library Ltd: A soldier reading out manifesto of Lenin's Order to peasants promising distribution of land and all belongings of landowners, March 2, 1917, manifesto, Russian Revolution, Russia, 20th century / De Agostini Picture Library / G. Dagli Orti 68tr
Getty Images: Ann Ronan Pictures / Print Collector 56br, Archiv Gerstenberg / ullstein bild 27tr, Corbis 43, DeAgostini / G. Dagli Orti 39bc, Fine Art Images / Heritage Images 9br, 64, 66tr, 90t, 101bl, Hulton Archive 17cr, Hulton-Deutsch Collection / Corbis 87, Keystone 58br, Laski Diffusion / East News 57cl, Slava Katamidze Collection 20tr, 75tr, Sovfoto / UIG 8cr, 12br, 16cr, 53c, ivbr, TASS 51br, Topical Press Agency 25, 90b, 103br, Universal History Archive / UIG 2, 29tr, 34c, 73br
Mary Evans Picture Library: INTERFOTO / Sammlung Rauch 31bc, John Massey Stewart Collection 35br
TopFoto: Fine Art Images / Heritage Images 14cr

All other images © Pearson Education

We are grateful to the following for permission to reproduce copyright material:

Text
Extract on page 54 and page 60 from *A People's Tragedy: The History of the Russian Revolution, 1891–1924*, Pimlico (Figes,O. 1997) copyright © 1996 by Orlando Figes. Used by permission of Penguin Random House Group and Viking Books, an imprint of Penguin Publishing Group, a division of Penguin Random House LLC. All rights and reserved; Extract on page 60 from *The Russian Revolution 1917–1921: A Short History*, Hodder Arnold Publication (White,J.D. 1994) reproduced by permission of Hodder Education.

Select glossary terms have been taken from *The Longman Dictionary of Contemporary English Online.*

Disclaimer
All maps in this book are drawn to support the key learning points. They are illustrative in style and are not exact representations.

Endorsement Statement
In order to ensure that this resource offers high-quality support for the associated Pearson qualification, it has been through a review process by the awarding body. This process confirms that this resource fully covers the teaching and learning content of the specification or part of a specification at which it is aimed. It also confirms that it demonstrates an appropriate balance between the development of subject skills, knowledge and understanding, in addition to preparation for assessment.

Endorsement does not cover any guidance on assessment activities or processes (e.g. practice questions or advice on how to answer assessment questions), included in the resource nor does it prescribe any particular approach to the teaching or delivery of a related course.

While the publishers have made every attempt to ensure that advice on the qualification and its assessment is accurate, the official specification and associated assessment guidance materials are the only authoritative source of information and should always be referred to for definitive guidance.

Pearson examiners have not contributed to any sections in this resource relevant to examination papers for which they have responsibility.

Examiners will not use endorsed resources as a source of material for any assessment set by Pearson. Endorsement of a resource does not mean that the resource is required to achieve this Pearson qualification, nor does it mean that it is the only suitable material available to support the qualification, and any resource lists produced by the awarding body shall include this and other appropriate resources.

ABOUT THIS BOOK

This book is written for students following the Pearson Edexcel International GCSE (9–1) History specification and covers one unit of the course. This unit is Russia and the Soviet Union, 1905–24, one of the Historical Investigations.

The History course has been structured so that teaching and learning can take place in any order, both in the classroom and in any independent learning. The book contains five chapters which match the five areas of content in the specification:
- Tsarist rule in Russia, 1905–14
- Opposition to Tsarist rule 1914–17: the impact of war and the February Revolution
- Provisional Government and the Bolshevik Revolution
- The Bolshevik consolidation of power and the Civil War
- War Communism and the New Economic Policy (NEP)

Each chapter is split into multiple sections to break down content into manageable chunks and to ensure full coverage of the specification.

Each chapter features a mix of learning and activities. Sources are embedded throughout to develop your understanding and exam-style questions help you to put learning into practice. Recap pages at the end of each chapter summarise key information and let you check your understanding. Exam guidance pages help you prepare confidently for the exam.

Learning objectives
Each section starts with a list of what you will learn in it. They are carefully tailored to address key assessment objectives central to the course.

Timeline
Visual representation of events to clarify the order in which they happened.

Key term
Useful words and phrases are colour coded within the main text and picked out in the margin with concise and simple definitions. These help understanding of key subject terms and support students whose first language is not English.

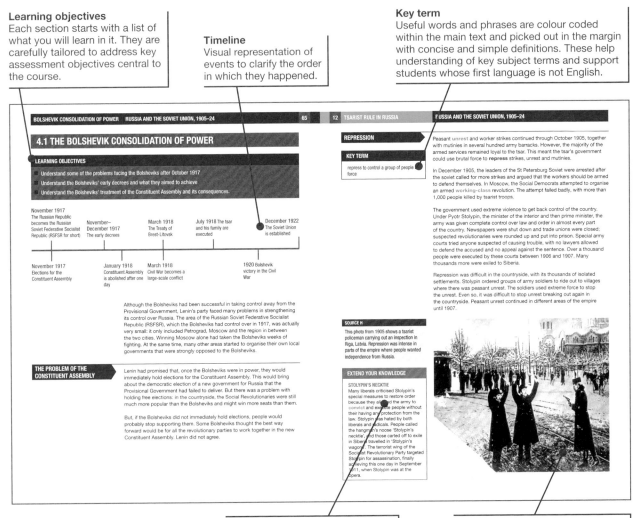

Extend your knowledge
Interesting facts to encourage wider thought and stimulate discussion. They are closely related to key issues and allow you to add depth to your knowledge and answers.

Source
Photos, cartoons and text sources are used to explain events and show you what people from the period said, thought or created, helping you to build your understanding.

Activity
Each chapter includes activities to help check and embed knowledge and understanding.

Recap
At the end of each chapter, you will find a page designed to help you consolidate and reflect on the chapter as a whole.

Recall quiz
This quick quiz is ideal for checking your knowledge or for revision.

Exam-style question
Questions tailored to the Pearson Edexcel specification to allow for practice and development of exam writing technique. They also allow for practice responding to the command words used in the exams.

Skills
Relevant exam questions have been assigned the key skills which you will gain from undertaking them, allowing for a strong focus on particular academic qualities. These transferable skills are highly valued in further study and the workplace.

Hint
All exam-style questions are accompanied by a hint to help you get started on an answer.

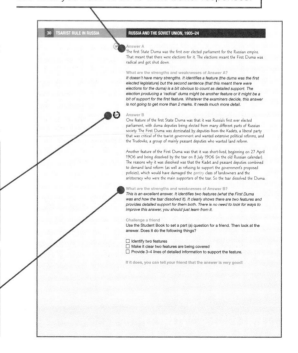

Checkpoint
Checkpoints help you to check and reflect on your learning. The Strengthen section helps you to consolidate knowledge and understanding, and check that you have grasped the basic ideas and skills. The Challenge questions push you to go beyond just understanding the information, and into evaluation and analysis of what you have studied.

Summary
The main points of each chapter are summarised in a series of bullet points. These are great for embedding core knowledge and handy for revision.

Exam guidance
At the end of each chapter, you will find two pages designed to help you better understand the exam questions and how to answer them. Each exam guidance section focuses on a particular question type that you will find in the exam, allowing you to approach them with confidence.

Student answers
Exemplar student answers are used to show what an answer to the exam question may look like. There are often two levels of answers so you can see what you need to do to write better responses.

Advice on answering the question
Three key questions about the exam question are answered here in order to explain what the question is testing and what you need to do to succeed in the exam.

Pearson Progression
Sample student answers have been given a Pearson step from 1 to 12. This tells you how well the response has met the criteria in the Pearson Progression Map.

Commentary
Feedback on the quality of the answer is provided to help you understand their strengths and weaknesses and show how they can be improved.

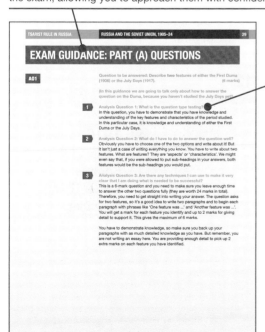

TIMELINE – RUSSIA AND THE SOVIET UNION, 1905–24

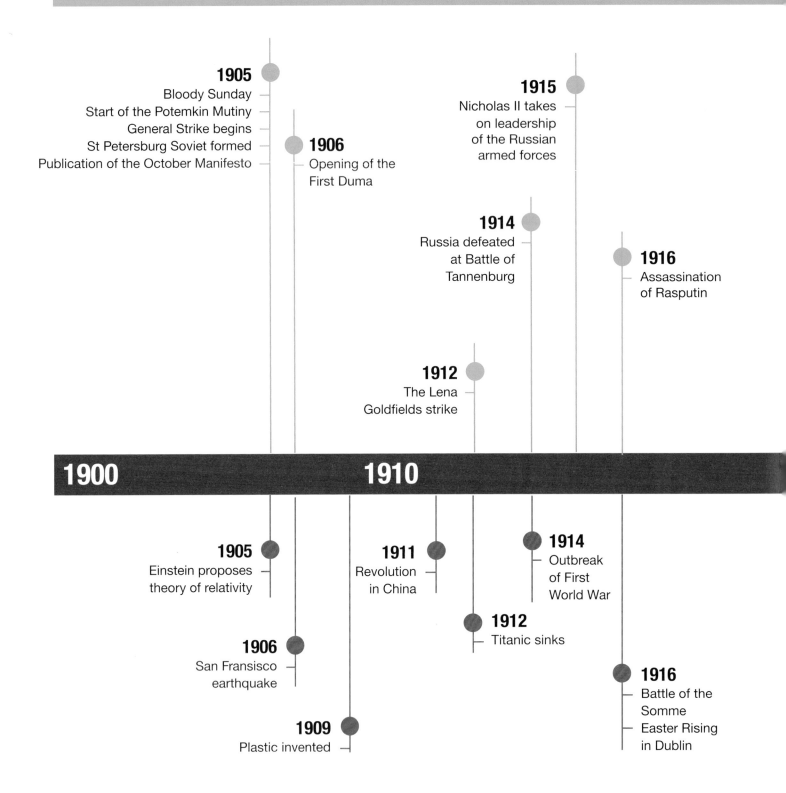

1905
Bloody Sunday
Start of the Potemkin Mutiny
General Strike begins
St Petersburg Soviet formed
Publication of the October Manifesto

1906
Opening of the
First Duma

1915
Nicholas II takes
on leadership
of the Russian
armed forces

1914
Russia defeated
at Battle of
Tannenburg

1916
Assassination
of Rasputin

1912
The Lena
Goldfields strike

1900

1910

1905
Einstein proposes
theory of relativity

1911
Revolution
in China

1914
Outbreak
of First
World War

1906
San Fransisco
earthquake

1912
Titanic sinks

1909
Plastic invented

1916
Battle of the
Somme
Easter Rising
in Dublin

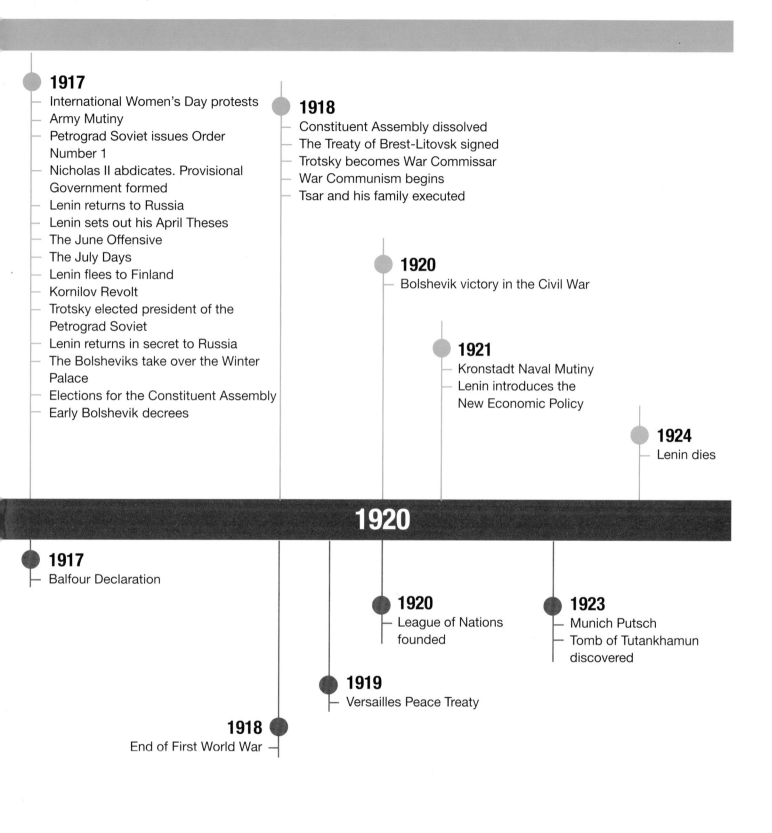

1917
- International Women's Day protests
- Army Mutiny
- Petrograd Soviet issues Order Number 1
- Nicholas II abdicates. Provisional Government formed
- Lenin returns to Russia
- Lenin sets out his April Theses
- The June Offensive
- The July Days
- Lenin flees to Finland
- Kornilov Revolt
- Trotsky elected president of the Petrograd Soviet
- Lenin returns in secret to Russia
- The Bolsheviks take over the Winter Palace
- Elections for the Constituent Assembly
- Early Bolshevik decrees

1918
- Constituent Assembly dissolved
- The Treaty of Brest-Litovsk signed
- Trotsky becomes War Commissar
- War Communism begins
- Tsar and his family executed

1920
- Bolshevik victory in the Civil War

1921
- Kronstadt Naval Mutiny
- Lenin introduces the New Economic Policy

1924
- Lenin dies

1920

1917
- Balfour Declaration

1920
- League of Nations founded

1923
- Munich Putsch
- Tomb of Tutankhamun discovered

1919
- Versailles Peace Treaty

1918
End of First World War

1. TSARIST RULE IN RUSSIA, 1905–14

LEARNING OBJECTIVES

- Understand the key features of tsarist rule in Russia in 1905, and reasons for discontent with tsarist rule
- Understand the key features of the 1905 revolution and its consequences
- Understand how Nicholas treated the dumas and the reasons for the growth of opposition groups.

In 1905 a violent revolution ripped through Russian society, briefly uniting most of the country and its empire against the ruler of the empire, the tsar, and his government. Even though revolutionary groups were operating within Russia, this revolution took them completely by surprise: it wasn't planned or led by revolutionaries, it was a sudden expression of people's unhappiness with 'the system'. The tsar managed to survive the revolution, although he was forced into allowing Russia's first-ever elected parliament. But after the tsar's army and police had brought Russia back under control, the tsar was anxious to side-line the new parliament and rule, as each tsar had always done, as the absolute, unlimited ruler of 'all the Russias' – his enormous empire.

1.1 TSARIST RULE IN 1905: REASONS FOR DISCONTENT

LEARNING OBJECTIVES

■ Understand the key features of tsarist rule in Russia in 1905

■ Explain the reasons for discontent with tsarist rule

■ Understand how the tsar tried to deal with opposition to his rule.

HOW WAS RUSSIA RULED?

KEY TERM

autocrat a ruler who has absolute power over a country

TSAR NICHOLAS II

By 1905 Russia had been ruled by one family, called the Romanovs, for nearly 300 years. Nicholas Romanov (Nicholas II) was **tsar** in 1905. He was 37 years old. Although he was the eldest son, Nicholas was never prepared for being tsar by his father, Alexander III. Nicholas could not cope with the demands of ruling Russia's huge **empire**. He was devoted to his family, but was a weak person who found it hard to make decisions, who had no patience for detail and few strong ideas of his own. The one idea Nicholas did believe strongly in was that he must pass on his powers as tsar to his son, as he had been passed them by his father and ancestors. He said, 'I will preserve the principle of **Autocracy** as firmly and unflinchingly as my late father.'

AUTOCRACY

Nicholas II ruled as an **autocrat**, which meant there were absolutely no controls on his power: no one could tell him what to do, or stop him doing what he wanted. The tsar was helped in his rule of the Russian empire by ministers, whom he could ask for advice. The tsar chose his ministers from the **aristocracy** and from senior Church leaders. The tsar was also in command of the armed services. All the army and navy swore personal loyalty to the tsar and the royal family.

Russia was a major European power in 1905, like Britain. Britain also had a king, but the real power was held by the British government. The government was formed from the political party that won the most votes in a general election. In Britain, people blamed the government for economic problems or an unpopular war, and could vote in a new government in the next general election. There was nothing like that in Russia. People did not usually criticise the tsar as they felt this was not loyal; they feared arrest if they developed a reputation for **opposition** to the tsar. If things were going badly, then it was assumed that the tsar's ministers must be giving him bad advice. But there was nothing they could do to change their government or how the tsar chose to rule.

REASONS FOR DISCONTENT

Different social groups in the Russian empire had different reasons to be discontented with the **tsarist** government.

SOURCE A

This photo of Nicholas II and his family was taken in 1905. His wife was called Alexandra. In the photo she is holding their son, the **heir to the throne**, who was called Alexei. Alexei was born in 1904. Nicholas had four daughters, who were called Anastasia, Olga, Tatiana and Maria.

EXTRACT A

From a biography of Nicholas II, published in 1990.

When, in 1894, he learned that he was to become tsar, Nicholas burst into tears. 'Oh Sandro,' he said to his cousin, 'I am not ready to be Tsar,' and he continued to sob bitterly.

His dream had been to be a sailor, to travel, to go on voyages round the world. Instead, he would have to attend Councils of Ministers, read reports, decide, govern, act.

ACTIVITY

What can you learn about Tsar Nicholas from Extract A?

Peasants – hungry for land, overtaxed, desperate poverty

Industrial workers – terrible working and living conditions, low pay, unemployment

Radicals – wanted the peasants or workers to take power for themselves

Reasons for discontent in 1905

Police state – no one could feel free because the police were always watching

Nationalities – parts of the Empire wanted to be independent, free from Russian oppression

Middle classes – no say in how Russia was governed

▶ **Figure 1.1** Key reasons for discontent in 1905

▼ SOCIAL GROUP	▼ REASONS FOR DISCONTENT
Peasants	Around 85 per cent of the population of the Russian empire were peasants. Population growth meant peasants needed more land, but almost all were too poor to buy it. Famines in the 1890s and in 1901 killed thousands. Russians were very shocked at how badly the government dealt with the famines: in fact, the Russian word for famine was banned from newspapers by the government!
Industrial workers	Russia had only really started industrialising in the 1890s, so the number of industrial workers was small. However, heavy industry was growing fast, concentrated in huge factories in Russia's major cities. Conditions in the factories were dangerous, working hours were long, pay was low, rules were strictly enforced and housing shortages meant workers were forced to live in overcrowded, dirty barracks where diseases spread rapidly.
Middle classes	Most of Russia's middle-class people were liberals. They wanted to see changes in Russia, but were frightened of the radical revolutionary groups that wanted to share all property among the poor. Many thought the best way to prevent revolution was not with violence, but by replacing the tsarist regime with a constitution that guaranteed rights to everyone, under a fair legal system.
Non-Russians	A census in 1897 recorded 125 million people in the Russian empire, of which only 44 per cent were Russian by nationality. Some of the other nationalities wanted independence because the empire put Russia first in everything. The empire had a policy of 'Russification', which put pressure on other nationalities to speak Russian and adopt Russian culture. The policy had most of its support among the peasants.

KEY TERMS

liberal a person who believes in freedom from too much control by the state. Freedom of speech and the right to vote are important liberal values

radical (adj) having ideas that are very new and different, and against what most people think or believe

constitution a written document that sets out how a country is governed

KEY TERM

socialist a person who thinks the state should own important industries and share the wealth created by these industries among everyone

A RADICAL THREAT

Tsarism had been under direct attack from revolutionaries. In 1881, Nicholas' grandfather, Alexander II, was assassinated; through the early 1900s, terrorists also assassinated important government ministers. Most of these terrorists belonged to the Socialist Revolutionary Party (or the SRs for short). The terrorists believed that the tsarist government deserved to be destroyed through violence. Some of these revolutionaries followed socialist theory. **Socialists** believed that Russia would eventually have a revolution in which the workers would take control.

One organisation called the Russian Social Democratic Party (RSDP) had formed in 1898. It followed the ideas of Karl Marx, a German revolutionary socialist. Its membership was tiny. One part of the membership, called the Mensheviks, believed it would be a long time until Russia had industrialised enough to have a workers' revolution. The other part, known as the Bolsheviks, believed in leading a workers' revolution as soon as the time seemed right. The Bolsheviks were led by Vladimir Ulyanov. Political parties were illegal and radicals adopted new names to hide their identities from the police. Vladimir Ulyanov called himself Lenin.

Vladimir Lenin's police record, made on his arrest in Moscow in 1896.

THE POLICE STATE

In order to protect the tsar and the government from the threat of terrorism, the police were given a great deal of power. The courts and the police served the tsarist autocracy, not the people of the Russian empire. Censorship of books and newspapers prevented radical ideas from being published. People suspected of working against the regime were imprisoned or exiled to Siberia, the remote east of the Russian empire. Lenin may have called himself after the Lena River, a Siberian river crossed by many exiles.

A secret police division, called the Okhrana, kept watch on people suspected by the regime of being revolutionaries. Okhrana agents also pretended to be revolutionaries so they could find out what underground groups were planning. Terrorists who were caught were usually executed. One terrorist who was executed was Lenin's brother, Alexander.

ACTIVITY

1 In groups of three, come up with three slogans to reflect what the peasants, the workers and the middle classes disliked about tsarism. Write them in graffiti-style lettering and post them up around the class.
2 Design a set of questions you could ask, as an undercover tsarist police agent, to see if your friends had come under the influence of revolutionary parties with extreme views.
3 Describe two key features of tsarism in 1905 that were reasons for discontent within the Russian empire.

1.2 CAUSES AND CONSEQUENCES OF THE 1905 REVOLUTION

LEARNING OBJECTIVES

■ Understand key features of the 1905 revolution

■ Understand the events and consequences of the revolution

■ Explain the reasons why Tsar Nicholas II survived the revolution.

IMMEDIATE CAUSES OF THE REVOLUTION

The general discontent with tsarist rule can be seen as the long-term causes of the 1905 revolution. This discontent meant pressure was building up against the harsh conditions and lack of freedom in tsarist Russia. In 1905, two important events helped provide the immediate causes of the revolution.

THE RUSSO–JAPANESE WAR, 1904–05

Russia wanted control of a part of northern China called Manchuria. This region had valuable resources (including coal and silver) and, most important of all, a port where the sea did not freeze over in winter (unlike Russian ports). However, Japan also had plans for Manchuria and this led to a war between Russia and Japan in 1904. Russia was confident that, as a major European power, it could easily beat Japan. However, the Japanese defeated the old-fashioned military tactics of the Russians both on land and at sea. Russian people blamed the tsarist government for this embarrassing defeat.

BLOODY SUNDAY

Bloody Sunday was a massacre of unarmed protesters that took place in St Petersburg on Sunday 9 January 1905. A large crowd of protesters, led by a priest called Father Gapon, was bringing a petition to the tsar. The protesters were factory workers and their families. The petition, signed by 150,000 people, called for an 8-hour working day, the right to organise trade unions and for a constitution to guarantee these rights and other freedoms in law.

EXTEND YOUR KNOWLEDGE

THE BATTLE OF TSUSHIMA, 14–15 MAY 1905

Russia sent its Baltic Fleet to East Asia to fight Japan; it was a journey of nearly 3,000 km. Starting in October 1904, the fleet took over 7 months to reach the East China Sea. As the Baltic Fleet was steaming through the Tsushima Strait, a stretch of sea leading to the Sea of Japan, the Japanese fleet attacked. The Russian ships were older and less manoeuvrable than the Japanese ships, and the Russians had not had time to keep their ships in good condition after such a long journey. The Russian fleet was crushed in the battle, with Russia losing all its battleships, 5,000 men killed and 5,000 captured.

SOURCE C

From the petition carried by the protesters to the tsar's palace in St Petersburg on 9 January 1905 (Bloody Sunday).

We, workers and inhabitants of the city of St. Petersburg..., our wives, children, and helpless old parents, have come to you, Sovereign, to seek justice and protection. We are impoverished and oppressed, we are burdened with work, and insulted. We are treated not like humans [but] like slaves... We have suffered, but we only get pushed deeper and deeper into a gulf of misery, ignorance, and lack of rights.

Sovereign, we have no strength left. We have reached the limit of our patience... And so we left our work and declared to our employers that we will not return to work until they meet our demands.

ACTIVITY

What does Source C tell us about why the Bloody Sunday protesters were discontented? Were their complaints to the tsar political or economic, or a mixture?

Although the protest **march** was peaceful, the way to the tsar's palace was blocked by soldiers. The demonstrators shouted abuse at the soldiers, including insults about military failures in Manchuria. The soldiers fired two rounds of warning shots. Mounted Cossacks, the regime's elite **troops**, charged into the crowd, attacking with their **whips** and then with swords. The soldiers fired into the crowd. Over 100 protesters were killed and hundreds more wounded. Around the world, people were shocked by the massacre. In Russia, the events of Bloody Sunday united people in anger and disgust at the actions of the tsarist government.

SOURCE D

From a report about Bloody Sunday written by US diplomats in Russia the day after the massacre.

In all the years (eighteen) I have spent in Russia, I never knew the Russian public to be so united as in their views in connection with the action of the authorities in ordering the soldiers to shoot the workmen, their wives, children and harmless spectators last Sunday in St Petersburg. All classes condemn the authorities and more particularly the Emperor. The present ruler has lost absolutely the affection of the Russian people, and whatever the future may have in store for the dynasty, the present Czar will never again be safe in the midst of his people.

SOURCE E

A contemporary illustration of Bloody Sunday: the troops have just fired on the protesters.

EXAM-STYLE QUESTION

A01

Describe **two** features of the Bloody Sunday massacre of 1905.   **(6 marks)**

HINT

Support your identification of a key feature with details from your knowledge.

THE EVENTS OF THE 1905 REVOLUTION

KEY TERM

mutiny a rebellion in the army of navy against someone in charge

POTEMKIN MUTINY, JUNE 1905

Although most of Russia's military forces remained loyal to the tsar in 1905, there were some **mutinies**. The most famous is the mutiny by sailors of the Russian navy battleship *Potemkin*.

Like the industrial workers, the sailors in the Russian navy faced very tough discipline and very poor conditions. As with the industrial workers, there were some sailors who had learned about socialism. They believed it was wrong for officers to have complete control over the lives of ordinary sailors, just because they were from the **upper classes**. The navy was also suffering from low confidence because of its embarrassing defeat by Japan in the Battle of Tsushima in May 1905.

The **quartermaster** of the battleship *Potemkin* was a socialist called Matyushenko. He and other crewmen planned to lead a mutiny of the Black Sea Fleet (the main part of Russia's navy) that would link up with the peasants of the Russian empire to bring down the tsar.

On 14 June 1905, *Potemkin*'s cooks reported that the meat for the crew's meal was full of maggots. The ship's doctor inspected the meat and said it was of acceptable quality for the men. After more complaints, *Potemkin*'s **executive officer** threatened to shoot any sailors who refused to eat the meat. When the sailors continued to disobey orders, the officer shot one of the leading mutineers, who died soon after. This set off the *Potemkin* mutiny. Other sailors grabbed the officer who had fired the shot, threw him into the water and shot him. Then the sailors attacked the rest of the officers, killing some and locking up others, and took control of the ship. A socialist 'people's committee' took control of the battleship, with Matyushenko as its chairperson.

The mutineers sailed *Potemkin* to the port of Odessa, where strikes and protests had been taking place for several weeks. There were demonstrations in support of the mutiny and large crowds attended the funerals of sailors killed by the ship's officers. Riots spread through the city. Nicholas II ordered the army in Odessa to stop the riots, which they did by firing into the crowds. Over 1,000 citizens were killed. The city was brought under government control again.

Shortly afterwards, an attempt to spread the mutiny through the rest of the Black Sea Fleet failed, and *Potemkin* was forced to sail around the Black Sea, avoiding recapture and looking for supplies. On 8 July 1905, *Potemkin* entered the Romanian port of Constanta, where the mutineers were given asylum. They sank the ship rather than allow the Russian government to recapture it.

This portrayal of the *Potemkin* mutiny was painted in 1952. It shows the moment when the sailors attacked their officers to take control of the ship, following the shooting of Grigory Vakulinchuk, a leading mutineer.

EXTEND YOUR KNOWLEDGE

THE BATTLESHIP *POTEMKIN*
In the Soviet Union, the *Potemkin* mutineers were seen as revolutionary heroes who helped set the Russian empire on its course towards the revolutions of 1917. A film called *The Battleship Potemkin* was made in 1925 to celebrate the mutiny. The importance of Bolshevik revolutionaries in the mutiny was stressed, but this was not a major feature of the mutiny itself.

ACTIVITY

1 You have been asked to give a short radio report on one feature of the *Potemkin* mutiny. You have to speak for exactly 20 seconds. What feature would you choose and what information would you use to support it? Does your report last exactly 20 seconds?
2 Explain why rebellions within the military were particularly worrying to the tsarist government.
3 Storyboard the events of the *Potemkin* mutiny. How might a tsarist film of the mutiny have presented the key events?

PEASANTS AND WORKERS IN THE 1905 REVOLUTION

The crisis that followed Bloody Sunday featured great waves of protest in the countryside and in the industrial cities.

PEASANT RIOTS
Across the Russian countryside, peasants rioted against their landlords, often burning down their manor houses (3,000 were burnt down between 1905 and 1907) and sometimes killing landlords and their families. The peasants created communes by taking the land that their parents and grandparents had worked as serfs. The police and army had great difficulty trying to deal with the number of attacks which broke out.

INDUSTRIAL WORKERS
While peasants tried to take control of land through violence and threats, industrial workers used strikes to achieve their aims. Bloody Sunday led to a huge increase in the number of strikes: more than 400,000 workers went on strike in January 1905 alone.

A general strike was organised from 20 September to 2 October 1905. Workers from the most important industries, including the railway, joined the strike. Without railways to transport resources, information and people, Russia was not able to function. The general strike linked the workers with the liberal middle classes, who wanted political reform. The protests united Russians against oppression; the general strike became a national strike against the government.

EXTEND YOUR KNOWLEDGE

The first soviet ever was created in a Moscow textile factory in the middle of May 1905.

THE ST PETERSBURG SOVIET
The word 'soviet' means council in Russian. The St Petersburg Soviet was a council of workers set up in October 1905 to help organise the general strike in the city. Other soviets were set up in other cities also to organise major strikes. The St Petersburg Soviet lasted only from September to early December, when the government shut it down, and it was not responsible for the general strike itself – it formed after the general strike had already begun. But it was a very important development: the idea of a workers' soviet for organising resistance and revolution became important again in 1917, as did the chairperson of the St Petersburg Soviet, Lev Trotsky.

THE OCTOBER MANIFESTO

KEY TERMS

concession agreeing to something that would not usually be allowed

freedom of speech/religion the right to say things or follow a religion without being treated unfairly by the government

trade union an organisation of workers that can bargain on the workers' behalf with employers for better pay and working conditions

ACTIVITY

1 Describe two key features of the 1905 revolution that you think were important in forcing Nicholas to agree to the October Manifesto.

2 'For the workers and peasants the 1905 revolution was a failure, while for the middle classes it was a success.' Come up with two points to support this statement, and one point that argues against it.

3 In Source G, the figure being carried on someone's shoulders is carrying a set of open manacles (chains used to secure prisoners' legs or arms). Why do you think the painter included this detail?

The pressure of the general strike and increasingly worrying signs of mutiny in the army led to Nicholas' ministers advising him to make **concessions**. Although they did not approve of giving in to violence and opposition, these ministers knew that something had to be done to restore order. The result was the October Manifesto.

The October Manifesto was published on 17 October 1905. In it, the tsar granted:

- new civil rights for the people of the Russian empire: **freedom of speech**, **freedom of religion**, the right to form political parties and the right to form **trade unions**
- a parliament, known as duma, with representatives elected in a general election
- that any new laws would have to be approved by the State Duma and government actions would be supervised by elected representatives of the people.

IMMEDIATE REACTIONS TO THE OCTOBER MANIFESTO

The October Manifesto delighted the liberal middle classes. The general strike was called off. There were widespread celebrations.

SOURCE G

This picture, called *17 October 1905*, was painted by the Russian painter Ilya Repin. It shows the delighted reaction on the streets to the announcement of the October Manifesto. Repin himself had taken part in many demonstrations against the government during 1905.

However, the October Manifesto did not do anything to improve conditions for the workers or peasants, or those suffering tough discipline in the armed services. The Social Democrats were very critical of the October Manifesto and of the middle classes for abandoning the workers.

REPRESSION

KEY TERM

repress to control a group of people by force

Peasant **unrest** and worker strikes continued through October 1905, together with mutinies in several hundred army barracks. However, the majority of the armed services remained loyal to the tsar. This meant the tsar's government could use brutal force to **repress** strikes, unrest and mutinies.

In December 1905, the leaders of the St Petersburg Soviet were arrested after the soviet called for more strikes and argued that the workers should be armed to defend themselves. In Moscow, the Social Democrats attempted to organise an armed **working-class** revolution. The attempt failed badly, with more than 1,000 people killed by tsarist troops.

The government used extreme violence to get back control of the country. Under Pyotr Stolypin, the minister of the interior and then prime minister, the army was given complete control over law and order in almost every part of the country. Newspapers were shut down and trade unions were closed; suspected revolutionaries were rounded up and put into prison. Special army courts tried anyone suspected of causing trouble, with no lawyers allowed to defend the accused and no appeal against the sentence. Over a thousand people were executed by these courts between 1906 and 1907. Many thousands more were exiled to Siberia.

Repression was difficult in the countryside, with its thousands of isolated settlements. Stolypin ordered groups of army soldiers to ride out to villages where there was peasant unrest. The soldiers used extreme force to stop the unrest. Even so, it was difficult to stop unrest breaking out again in the countryside. Peasant unrest continued in different areas of the empire until 1907.

SOURCE H

This photo from 1905 shows a tsarist policeman carrying out an inspection in Riga, Latvia. Repression was intense in parts of the empire where people wanted independence from Russia.

EXTEND YOUR KNOWLEDGE

STOLYPIN'S NECKTIE
Many liberals criticised Stolypin's special measures to restore order because they allowed the army to **convict** and execute people without their having any protection from the law. Stolypin was hated by both liberals and radicals. People called the hangman's noose 'Stolypin's necktie', and those carted off to exile in Siberia travelled in 'Stolypin's wagons'. The terrorist wing of the Socialist Revolutionary Party targeted Stolypin for assassination, finally achieving this one day in September 1911, when Stolypin was at the opera.

REASONS WHY NICHOLAS II SURVIVED THE 1905 REVOLUTION

Lenin wrote that the 1905 revolution was a 'dress rehearsal' for a revolution: it had many of the features of a revolution but it did not achieve its aim, which was to **overthrow** the tsar. Why *did* Nicholas survive in 1905?

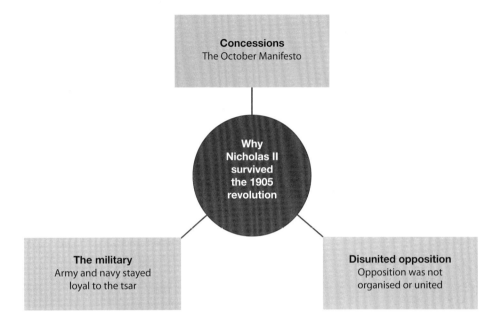

▶ Figure 1.2 Reasons why Nicholas II survived the 1905 revolution

THE OCTOBER MANIFESTO

Although tsarism came close to completely losing control of Russia during the general strike in the autumn of 1905, it managed to survive by promising the reforms that liberal middle-class people demanded. For the middle classes, this was as much revolution as they wanted. The October Manifesto split those wanting reform from those wanting wider revolution, so it reduced the pressure on the tsar.

THE MILITARY

Tsar Nicholas II was generally able to rely on his armed services to defend him from the revolution. Mutinies were quite unusual. Once the Russo–Japanese War ended in 1905, tsarist troops could be used to deal with worker or peasant unrest. Nicholas also arranged for a large loan from France, which he used to pay his armed forces. This improved confidence and helped make sure the troops remained loyal.

A DISUNITED OPPOSITION

Opponents of tsarism were not united. Much of the unrest was spontaneous, meaning that it wasn't planned. Most of it was about economic issues, too, rather than being about achieving specific political goals: people in the cities wanted cheaper bread; peasants wanted more land; workers wanted more pay and easier working conditions.

The Social Democrats thought this showed how workers and peasants were not educated enough to understand that only a political revolution could give them what they wanted. They felt it was therefore the responsibility of revolutionary parties, like the Bolsheviks, to lead the way.

KEY TERM

anarchy a situation in which there is no government control at all and everyone is free to do whatever they want

SOURCE I

This illustration from 1905 shows how some Russians saw the revolution: terrifying violence that threatened to bring **anarchy** to Russia.

МОСКВА
I.

Б. М. Кустодиев.

ВСТУПЛЕНІЕ.

EXTEND YOUR KNOWLEDGE

NICHOLAS II AND THE SURVIVAL OF TSARISM

The tsar did very little for himself to save tsarism from the 1905 revolution. He was not really aware that a revolution was happening through most of 1905. His advisers regularly moved him around the country to keep him safe from assassination attempts. His favourite place was a summer holiday home outside St Petersburg, where he could enjoy walks and tea parties with his family. Nicholas could not understand requests to change the autocratic system, as he believed God wanted Russia to be ruled in this way.

EXAM-STYLE QUESTION

A01

Describe **two** features of Stolypin's policy of repression. **(6 marks)**

HINT

This question is about you demonstrating 'knowledge and understanding of the key features and characteristics of the periods studied'. So you have to make sure you provide good detailed *factual* support for your answer.

1.3 NICHOLAS AND THE DUMAS

LEARNING OBJECTIVES

■ Understand key features of the first four dumas

■ Understand the tsar's attitude to the dumas

■ Understand key features of Stolypin's land reform and the reasons for the growth of opposition groups.

Tsarism was in crisis in October 1905; Nicholas had been forced to promise to share his power with an elected parliament. However, by April 1906, when the government set out its political reforms in its Fundamental Laws, the tsar and his government were back in control.

THE FUNDAMENTAL LAWS, APRIL 1906

KEY TERMS

delegate someone who has been elected to vote for or take decisions for a group, a representative

veto the right to reject a decision made by parliament, such as a decision for a new law

dissolve when a parliament is dissolved, it means that parliament is ended and a new one has to be elected

These laws established Russia's State Duma, the first parliament of around 500 elected **delegates**. The duma had a real role in making new laws for Russia. However, the powers of the duma were limited.

■ The duma's powers were matched by an upper house of parliament, the Imperial State Council. The State Council could block anything passed by the duma. Half the State Council's members were chosen directly by the tsar and would always vote in the way the tsar wanted them to.

■ The tsar kept hold of very important powers. He alone had authority over the armed services and foreign policy. He chose all his government ministers. He had the right to **veto** any duma legislation. He had the power to **dissolve** the duma at any time (though he had to say when elections for the new duma would then take place). When the duma was not in operation, the tsar had the right to pass any new laws he thought necessary, under Article 87 of the Fundamental Laws.

■ Only the tsar was able to make changes to the Fundamental Laws of Russia.

NICHOLAS' ATTITUDE TO THE DUMA

The reasons for these limitations on the duma was that neither Nicholas nor his ministers trusted the idea of allowing the Russian people to have a say in how Russia and its empire should be governed. Nicholas hated the idea of limiting his sacred autocratic powers in any way, and believed deeply that the majority of the Russian people wanted him to remain as their absolute ruler. An elected duma could only be acceptable to the tsar if the duma could be counted on to support the tsar and his government.

At the same time, Nicholas and the government did treat the duma as important. The government encouraged people to celebrate the opening of the First Duma by decorating their homes and businesses with flags. After the opening ceremony, duma deputies went to the tsar's Winter Palace, where the tsar made a speech to them.

SOURCE J

From Nicholas II's speech to duma deputies, 27 April 1906.

Almighty God entrusted to My care the welfare of the Fatherland [Russia] and impelled Me to summon representatives of the people to assist in legislative activity making laws…

It is my firm conviction that your unselfish service to the Fatherland will help determine the needs of the peasants so near My heart, and contribute to the enlightenment of the people and the advancement of their welfare.

May My earnest desire be fulfilled: may I see My people happy and pass on to My Son, as his inheritance, a strong, well-ordered, and enlightened state.

May God bless the work confronting Me and the State Council and the State Duma.

SOURCE K

Tsar Nicholas II giving his speech to the deputies of the State Duma at the Winter Palace, St Petersburg, on 27 April 1906.

ACTIVITY

1 Which one of the following do you think best describes the tone used by the tsar towards the duma deputies?
  a Respectful: the tsar was appreciative and polite, and welcomed the duma deputies as men who would help with the urgent task of modernising Russia.
  b Dismissive: the tsar did not value their contribution, and warned the duma deputies they would have no real role in governing Russia so they should not get any big ideas.
  c Patronising: the arrogant tsar made it clear that the deputies were elected only by his permission and that their role was to help him understand his people better.
2 Select phrases from Source J to support the decision you made in Activity 1.

THE FIRST FOUR DUMAS AND OPPOSITION TO TSARISM

April to July 1906
First Duma

November 1907 to June 1912
Third Duma

February to June 1907
Second Duma

November 1912 to February 1917
Fourth Duma

Before 1905, political parties had been illegal in Russia. After 1905, many different parties formed, from **ultra-conservatives** like the Union of the Russian People to the extreme **left-wing** Russian Social Democratic Party. The two **middle-ground** political parties were the Constitutional Democrats (known as the Kadets) and the Octobrists (named after the October Manifesto). The Kadets were more liberal, while the Octobrists were more conservative.

EXTRACT B

From a history of Russia, published in 1981.

The first two Dumas proved to be bitter and unworkable experiments. Too many of the Duma deputies were completely opposed to the government, while Nicholas and his advisors regarded most of the Duma deputies as having evil intentions. Everyone assumed rigid, unyielding positions.

ACTIVITY

How do you know that the author of Extract B did not think that the duma was doing a good job?

SOURCE L

Five peasant deputies from the First Duma, 1906.

THE FIRST DUMA, 27 APRIL–8 JULY 1906

The left-wing revolutionary parties did not take part in the elections for the First Duma, but even without them the duma was strongly anti-government. It was dominated by deputies from the Kadets and the Trudoviks. The Socialist Revolutionary (SR) Party had refused to take part in the First Duma. The Trudoviks were SRs who disagreed about this and had split to form a new peasant party. Their main demand was land reform: taking more land from the landlords. The Kadets supported land reform, but also wanted the State Council to be abolished and for the government to answer directly to the duma.

These demands were far too radical for the tsarist government, but the duma deputies were not interested in any sort of compromise. So the tsar dissolved the First Duma after just 10 weeks. Liberals were extremely disappointed by this speedy return to autocracy. There was a strong increase in liberal opposition to the government.

THE SECOND DUMA, FEBRUARY–JUNE 1907

This time, the Socialist Revolutionary Party (the SRs) and the Social Democratic Party (RSDP) took part in the elections. Two hundred and twenty-two socialists, mostly SRs, were elected. The new prime minister, Pyotr Stolypin, soon realised that the Second Duma was even more of a threat to tsarism than the First Duma, and it was dissolved in June 1907. For the revolutionary parties, it became clear that they would not achieve their aims through elections.

THE THIRD AND FOURTH DUMAS, NOVEMBER 1907–FEBRUARY 1917

On 3 June 1907, Stolypin organised a change in the election rules so that more conservative deputies, rather than reformers, were elected to the Third Duma. Conservative deputies could usually be relied on to support the government. Stolypin's change meant that the Octobrists and other conservative deputies controlled 287 of the 443 duma seats. The liberals were very shocked that the government would act in such a dishonest way in order to control a duma. They now realised that the tsar and his government would never willingly give up autocratic power. Although opposition parties continued to make speeches in the duma criticising government actions, the conservatives always made sure government policies got duma support.

The Third Duma lasted its full 5-year term; the government did not need to close it down because it could be relied on to support the tsar's regime. The Fourth Duma, dominated also by conservatives, was similar to the Third Duma, except this time the right-wing, nationalist parties were even stronger. Again, opposition to the government was too weak to make an impact on laws or policies. The Fourth Duma lasted until February 1917.

A COUNTER-REVOLUTION?

By the time of the Third Duma, police repression was so severe that the revolutionary parties were almost unable to operate. It was difficult for the parties to connect with the workers, too; factory owners were allowed to sack striking workers, so those who had jobs were desperate to hold on to them and had to keep their distance from the revolutionaries. In the countryside, the peasants were also intimidated by Stolypin's repression. Landlords had fortified their manor houses, employed armed guards and, in some cases, installed searchlights to guard against night-time attacks. By rigging the elections, the Third Duma was packed with conservatives, most of them landlords who would never agree to radical land reforms. The Kadets, who had hoped to prevent revolution through social and political reforms, felt betrayed by the government, and exhausted by the 'whirlpool' of politics since 1906.

EXTEND YOUR KNOWLEDGE

THE BLACK HUNDREDS

Not all Russians opposed tsarism. Instead of blaming the tsar and the government for Russia's troubles, some extreme nationalist groups held others accountable, especially the Jewish communities. Known as the Black Hundreds, these extreme nationalist groups launched pogroms on those they opposed. More than 3,000 people, mostly Jews, were killed by the Black Hundreds between 1905 and 1906. While some government ministers criticised the Black Hundred attacks, there were strong links between the police and the Black Hundreds, and the latter were certainly important in helping the government regain control and repress the revolution. Nicholas II himself was convinced that Jews were responsible for the 1905 revolution.

ACTIVITY

1 The Octobrists, Kadets and Social Democrats had different fortunes in the years of the first three dumas. Use a graph like the one below to show how you think members of each party felt between 1905 (First Duma) and 1907 (Third Duma).

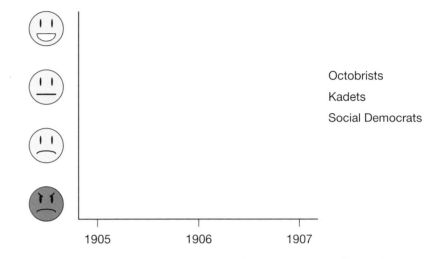

Octobrists

Kadets

Social Democrats

1905   1906   1907

2 Add annotations to your graph to explain the lines you have drawn.

STOLYPIN'S LAND REFORM

The peasant unrest against the landlords continued long after the cities were brought back under control. The Third Duma was packed with conservative landlords who wanted the countryside to be made 'safe' again. Prime Minister Stolypin came up with a solution.

THE 'WAGER ON THE STRONG'

Stolypin and the landlords did not want to give the peasants any more of their land. They argued that the inefficient, old-fashioned peasant communes would only waste it and peasants would stay as poor as before. This was because the commune controlled all the important decisions in the village: when to plough the land, which land should be used for which crops and how the land should be farmed. Even if a peasant wanted to do something new, the commune would not allow any change from the village traditions.

Stolypin's plan was to let individual peasants leave the commune and set up farms for themselves. There were different ways this could happen, but what Stolypin was hoping for was that Russia would soon become a country of individual family farms. As each farmer would get all the profits from his crops, rather than everything being shared with the commune, Stolypin hoped that his new farmers would use modern farming methods so they had more crops to sell.

Stolypin called it the 'wager on the strong'. Stolypin's wager was that if peasants became successful farmers, they would stop wanting to burn down their landlords' manor houses and start to support the government instead. Stolypin's reform also encouraged peasant migration to Siberia, where there was plenty of land. Between 1905 and 1917, 3.5 million peasants moved to Siberia.

SOURCE M

In this photo from 1906, two policemen stop a peasant from ploughing up his landlord's land. Stolypin's land reform wanted to make peasants into landowner-farmers, who would respect the landlord's property and look after their own private farms.

SOURCE N

From a description by Stolypin of his land reform.

If we were to provide the diligent [hard-working] farmer… with a separate plot of land…, making sure there was adequate water and that it satisfied all the other requirements for proper cultivation, then… there would arise an independent, prosperous husbandman [farmer], a stable citizen of the land.

SOURCE O

From a discussion between Stolypin and a conservative general, Kireev, in 1906.

Kireev: I rebuke you for the destruction of communal agriculture.

Stolypin: It is impossible not to abolish it! I have seen it, I know – and I know, too, the difference between it and landholding by [individual farmers]. Russia will immediately become richer.

Kireev: You have forgotten that it is not only a question of finances, but of politics. You are creating a mass of agricultural proletarians. All the peasants' land will be bought up by Jews.

Stolypin: So long as I am in post, that will not happen.

Kireev: Are you eternal, then?

KEY TERM

proletarian a member of the working class, those with nothing to survive on except their wages

ACTIVITY

1 In Source N, Stolypin talks about creating a 'stable citizen of the land'. Explain why Stolypin thought breaking up the peasant communes would make revolution less likely.

2 In Source O, Kireev argues that breaking up the communes would create 'a mass of agricultural **proletarians**'. Did this mean Kireev thought the reform would make revolution more or less likely? Explain your answer.

3 How far do you think Kireev agreed with Stolypin that the land reform would make Russia richer?

EXAM-STYLE QUESTION

A03

SKILLS   ANALYSIS, ADAPTIVE LEARNING, CREATIVITY

EXTEND YOUR KNOWLEDGE

DIFFERENT VIEWS OF STOLYPIN
In modern Russia, Stolypin is seen as one of Russia's greatest reformers who, if he had not been assassinated in 1911, could have saved Russia from the horrors of the revolutions, civil war and terror in the Soviet Union. Not all historians agree, though: some believed that Stolypin had upset almost everyone by 1911 and had no supporters either at court or in the duma; such conditions would have made it very difficult for him to continue his reform.

THE LENA GOLDFIELDS STRIKE

Study Sources N and O. How far does Source N support the evidence of Source O about the aims of Stolypin's land reform?
Explain your answer.   **(8 marks)**

HINT

Make sure you include both the ways in which the two sources agree, and the ways in which they disagree.

HOW SUCCESSFUL WAS THE LAND REFORM?

The land reform was very complex. Firstly, there were far more applications than the government had expected. Secondly, although in theory the peasants now had their own farms to run, in reality they and their families tended to work and live as though they were still part of a commune. For example, the strips of land owned by one peasant would be scattered across a much larger piece of field (divided into strips owned by different peasants); peasants continued to allow their animals to graze on each other's land.

By May 1915, only 14 per cent of peasants taking up the reform actually combined their land together in individual, enclosed family farms. It is possible that, had the reform continued, Stolypin would have succeeded in breaking up communes and creating individual farms on a much larger scale. However, his political aim of preventing further unrest in the countryside was unsuccessful. In 1917, peasant unrest once again swept through rural Russia, organised by the peasant communes that Stolypin had tried to break apart.

Stolypin's reform happened at the same time as his repressions of peasant unrest (see page 12) and worker strikes. There was constant police repression of trade unions and revolutionary groups. Then, in 1912, a year after Stolypin's assassination, there was a massacre of strikers at the Lena Goldfields in Siberia.

Working conditions for the gold miners along the Lena River had been terrible. One day, workers from one mining gang protested about the rotten horsemeat they were supposed to eat. This led to a strike (organised with help from the Bolsheviks) that spread through the goldfields. A number of strike leaders were arrested. The event turned into a mass protest of workers, who brought lists of their demands to the managers. As the huge crowd of protesters approached, troops fired into the crowd. Between 200 and 500 workers were killed, with hundreds more wounded.

The Lena Goldfields massacre kick-started a storm of protest throughout Russia. Repression meant the number of strikes had declined from thousands in 1905 to a few hundred in 1911. But after the massacre, there were nearly 2,000 strikes, and thousands of protest meetings. The duma organised an investigation into the massacre, led by Alexander Kerensky. He became famous for his reports about the terrible conditions endured by the miners. The reaction to the Lena Goldfields massacre showed that none of the reasons for discontent with tsarist rule had gone away. Instead of Russia moving towards better conditions and freedom, the tsar and his government continued to hold on to autocratic power, using the police and army to crush any opposition.

RECAP

RECALL QUESTIONS

1 What was the name of the family that had ruled Russia for nearly 300 years in 1905?
2 Who was the leader of the Bolshevik part of the Social Democratic Party in the period between 1905 and 1914?
3 Russia fought and lost a war against which country between 1904 and 1905?
4 In June 1905, a mutiny took place on an important battleship in Russia's Black Sea Fleet. What was the name of the ship?
5 What was set up in St Petersburg in September 1905 to help organise a general strike?
6 What did Article 87 of the Fundamental Laws give the tsar the power to do?
7 How many dumas were there between April 1906 and February 1917?
8 What did the term 'Kadet' stand for (a political party)?
9 What was Stolypin's 'wager on the strong'?
10 What happened in 1912 that made many people in Russia feel nothing had really changed in the way Russia was ruled since Bloody Sunday in 1905?

CHECKPOINT

STRENGTHEN

S1 Identify two reasons why Russians in 1905 were discontented with the tsarist government.
S2 What was 'Stolypin's necktie'? How was it linked to Stolypin's repression after the 1905 revolution?
S3 Explain three reasons why Nicholas II survived the 1905 revolution.

CHALLENGE

C1 Write a diary entry for Nicholas II, for 27 April 1906, describing his attitude towards the opening of the first State Duma.
C2 Suggest two reasons why it was difficult for the Bolsheviks to lead the opposition to the tsarist regime in the period between 1905 and 1914 (hint: their leader, Lenin, spent most of these years in exile in Switzerland).
C3 Make a list of the reasons you can find in this chapter to explain why Tsar Nicholas might have been unpopular.

SUMMARY

- The tsar ruled Russia as an autocrat.
- Russia was a major power but it had many weaknesses.
- Russia was defeated by Japan in war in 1905.
- In 1905, a revolution was brutally put down on Bloody Sunday.
- In 1905, sailors on the battleship *Potemkin* mutinied.
- The tsar issued the October Manifesto, granting concessions.
- Stolypin introduced land reform but also dealt severely with opposition to the tsar.
- The Fundamental Laws set up the dumas, which had limited powers.
- In 1911, Stolypin was assassinated.
- In 1912, the strike in the Lena Goldfields resulted in strikers being shot; discontent with the government increased.

EXAM GUIDANCE: PART (A) QUESTIONS

A01

Question to be answered: Describe **two** features of either the First Duma (1906) or the July Days (1917).   (6 marks)

(In this guidance we are going to talk only about how to answer the question on the Duma, because you haven't studied the July Days yet!)

1   Analysis Question 1: What is the question type testing?
In this question, you have to demonstrate that you have knowledge and understanding of the key features and characteristics of the period studied. In this particular case, it is knowledge and understanding of either the First Duma or the July Days.

2   Analysis Question 2: What do I have to do to answer the question well?
Obviously you have to choose one of the two options and write about it! But it isn't just a case of writing everything you know. You have to write about two features. What are features? They are 'aspects' or 'characteristics'. We might even say that, if you were allowed to put sub-headings in your answers, both features would be the sub-headings you would put.

3   Analysis Question 3: Are there any techniques I can use to make it very clear that I am doing what is needed to be successful?
This is a 6-mark question and you need to make sure you leave enough time to answer the other two questions fully (they are worth 24 marks in total). Therefore, you need to get straight into writing your answer. The question asks for two features, so it's a good idea to write two paragraphs and to begin each paragraph with phrases like 'One feature was ...' and 'Another feature was ...'. You will get a mark for each feature you identify and up to 2 marks for giving detail to support it. This gives the maximum of 6 marks.

You have to demonstrate knowledge, so make sure you back up your paragraphs with as much detailed knowledge as you have. But remember, you are not writing an essay here. You are providing enough detail to pick up 2 extra marks on each feature you have identified.

Answer A

The first State Duma was the first ever elected parliament for the Russian empire. That meant that there were elections for it. The elections meant the First Duma was radical and got shut down.

What are the strengths and weaknesses of Answer A?

It doesn't have many strengths. It identifies a feature (the duma was the first elected legislature) but the second sentence (that this meant there were elections for the duma) is a bit obvious to count as detailed support. The election producing a 'radical' duma might be another feature or it might be a bit of support for the first feature. Whatever the examiners decide, this answer is not going to get more than 2 marks. It needs much more detail.

Answer B

One feature of the first State Duma was that it was Russia's first ever elected parliament, with duma deputies being elected from many different parts of Russian society. The First Duma was dominated by deputies from the Kadets, a liberal party that was critical of the tsarist government and wanted extensive political reforms, and the Trudoviks, a group of mainly peasant deputies who wanted land reform.

Another feature of the First Duma was that it was short-lived, beginning on 27 April 1906 and being dissolved by the tsar on 8 July 1906 (in the old Russian calendar). The reasons why it was dissolved was that the Kadet and peasant deputies combined to demand land reform (as well as refusing to support the government's proposed policies), which would have damaged the gentry class of landowners and the aristocracy who were the main supporters of the tsar. So the tsar dissolved the Duma.

What are the strengths and weaknesses of Answer B?

This is an excellent answer. It identifies two features (what the First Duma was and how the tsar dissolved it). It clearly shows there are two features and provides detailed support for them both. There is no need to look for ways to improve this answer, you should just learn from it.

Challenge a friend

Use the Student Book to set a part (a) question for a friend. Then look at the answer. Does it do the following things?

☐ Identify two features
☐ Make it clear two features are being covered
☐ Provide 3–4 lines of detailed information to support the feature.

If it does, you can tell your friend that the answer is very good!

2. OPPOSITION TO TSARIST RULE, 1914–17

LEARNING OBJECTIVES

- Understand the economic, social and political effects of the First World War on Russia
- Understand the immediate causes of the February Revolution and its events
- Understand the events leading to the setting up of the Provisional Government.

The economic, social and political impacts of the First World War pushed Russia into chaos. Although Russia had the largest army in Europe, its millions of peasant army recruits had little training, few weapons (and even less ammunition) and very little food; they were ordered into battle by ill-informed commanders, only to be killed in their thousands by enemy machine guns. Faced with a string of military defeats, Tsar Nicholas II felt it was his duty to take personal command of the Russian army. However, as the defeats continued, Nicholas' decisions weakened his authority; his previous supporters, in both the military and the aristocracy, began to lose faith in him. Furthermore, control of the government was now left to his German wife, Alexandra, in Petrograd (the new name for St Petersburg). Alexandra was under the influence of Rasputin, a Russian monk whose shocking private life made the royal family look ridiculous. As a result, tsarism had few supporters by February 1917, when a revolution forced Nicholas to give up his throne.

2.1 THE EFFECTS OF THE FIRST WORLD WAR ON RUSSIA

LEARNING OBJECTIVES

■ Understand the economic effects of the First World War on Russia

■ Understand the social effects of the First World War on Russia

■ Understand the political effects of the First World War on Russia.

RUSSIA AND THE FIRST WORLD WAR

KEY TERMS

ally a country that agrees to help another country

mobilisation gathering together, organising and equipping an army and moving it towards the enemy

Russia was an **ally** of Serbia, so when tensions between Serbia and Austria led to war in 1914, Russia supported Serbia. Germany joined the war as an ally of Austria, which meant war for Russia against both Austria and Germany.

At first, the war gave tsarism a major boost. With Russia under threat, people felt very patriotic – they were proud of their country. The government proposed raising taxes to help pay for the war, and the duma supported this with a huge majority. The tsar's popularity increased, especially when the rapid **mobilisation** of Russia's huge army (the largest in the world in 1914) meant Russia was able to make advances into enemy territory.

However, Russia's early successes soon turned into terrible defeats. Germany was able to use its efficient railway system to move troops quickly to the best possible places to attack the Russians. After the first month of fighting, at the end of August 1914, the Germans won a stunning victory at Tannenburg. The Russians lost 122,000 men and vast quantities of supplies and weapons. Around 30,000 men were killed, the rest captured. The Russian commander was so ashamed of the scale of defeat that he committed suicide. More defeats quickly followed: two battles at the Masurian Lakes in September 1914 and February 1915 resulted in more heavy losses of men. By the end of 1915, Russia had lost 2 million men and was in retreat, with its enemies occupying three provinces of the Russian empire.

GROWING DISCONTENT

The military defeats led to growing discontent. This was not only sadness at the loss of so many Russian men, or anger at German occupation of Russian lands. People also blamed the tsarist government because there were not enough weapons and supplies for the army. One third of the army had no rifles. Men were ordered to charge unarmed at enemy machine guns, and pick up weapons from other soldiers who had been killed. The army was short of artillery shells and other ammunition. Soldiers did not have warm uniforms or boots for winter, and they did not have enough to eat. Russian citizens formed voluntary organisations to try to get supplies to the soldiers at the front, because they saw that the government could not manage it.

SOURCE A

Russian soldiers running away from a German attack on the Russian front lines.

NICHOLAS' DECISION TO TAKE COMMAND

In August 1915, Nicholas II decided that it was his duty to take command of the Russian army and navy, despite having no military experience. The tsar's ministers and the chairman of the duma all strongly advised Nicholas against this decision. They understood that, as commander-in-chief, the tsar would be blamed directly for any further military defeats. But Nicholas was determined. He believed it was his sacred duty to take responsibility for the defence of his country now it had been invaded; he felt this way he could focus both his government and his military on the defence of Russia.

SOURCE B

From an appeal by Nicholas' ministers asking him to rethink his decision to become commander-in-chief.

Sire, we make bold once more to tell you that, to the best of our understanding, your adoption of such a decision threatens Russia, yourself, and your dynasty with serious consequences.

ACTIVITY

1 Explain whether the following statements are true or false?
   a In 1914, Russia had the world's largest army.
   b One reason for Russia's defeats in 1914 was that it took its huge army much longer than expected to mobilise.
   c The war was unpopular in Russia from the start.
   d There was no good reason for the tsar to take command of the Russian forces.
2 Study Source B. Suggest three reasons why the tsar's ministers thought his decision to take command of Russia's armed forces was dangerous.

ECONOMIC EFFECTS OF THE FIRST WORLD WAR

The cost of the First World War was enormous: the Russian government spent 17 billion roubles on the war between 1914 and 1917, which was 15 times as much as it had spent on the Russo–Japanese War (see page 7). This time, Russia was less able to deal with the cost due to the ways in which the war had affected the Russian economy:

- The government had introduced prohibition (a ban on alcoholic drink) in 1914. This was to tackle the problem of drunkenness in Russian society. However, taxes from sales of vodka had made up an astonishing 25 per cent of the government's tax receipts, so now the government had to find money elsewhere by putting up other taxes and getting loans from other countries. The country's **national debt** increased.
- The regions captured by the Germans in the war included some of the empire's most important economic areas, for example, the coal-mining areas in what is now Poland. Germany also blocked Russia's access to Europe, making it impossible to trade with its allies. All imports and exports had to go through Vladivostok, Russia's port in the far east of Siberia (which also froze over in winter).
- The military demanded a ban on grain exports from Russia, so that they could take what they needed from peasant harvest for the soldiers.
- Over 15 million men were sent to fight in the war. This meant there was not enough labour for the factories or the fields. In 1915, over 500 factories had to close because there weren't enough workers and some fields were left without crops.

Faced with growing economic problems, the government decided to solve them by printing more money. This led to **inflation**. Although printing more money meant the government had more to use to pay off its debts, money itself became less valuable because there was so much more of it. Prices in shops went up, while wages remained low. People found that their bank savings were now worth a lot less than before.

KEY TERMS

national debt the total amount of money the government of a country has borrowed. Very high national debts worry international investors, meaning that they might stop investing in the country

inflation the increase in prices for goods

requisitioning taking something, e.g. food, from someone by official order. Food requisitioning meant taking as much grain from peasants as the army needed, at a fixed low price

SOCIAL EFFECTS OF THE FIRST WORLD WAR

Russia was able to increase its supply of weapons and ammunition by switching industrial production to military needs. The army was able, through **requisitioning**, to take the food it needed from peasant farmers to feed the soldiers on the front line. The railway system gave priority to transporting supplies to the army in the west. However, this focus on meeting military needs first had major social consequences.

- Not enough food was being produced to supply both the army and the cities. Railway transport focused only on getting food to the army, so food for the cities often sat in wagons until it rotted, since there were no trains to take it across Russia to cities where people were running out of food.
- Inflation meant that prices increased much faster than wages. Working-class people struggled to afford what little food was available. Middle-class people saw their savings becoming less and less valuable each day.
- During the war, the countryside lost so many men of working age to the army that, by 1916, there were twice as many women in the Russian countryside as there were men. Many of these families were also mourning the loss of relatives or friends killed in the war.
- In the cities, the number of jobs fell sharply because the factories lost their overseas markets and could not get enough raw materials delivered by rail to keep production going. In the first 3 months of the war, 150,000 workers had lost their jobs completely or been sent home because of there being no work for them to do.

EXTRACT A

From a history of Russia, published in 1986.

What struck most savagely at the soldiers' morale and pushed the workers beyond the point of endurance was the shortage of food. The government could do nothing. Ministers watched helplessly as grain reserves dropped to dangerously low levels.

ACTIVITY

How does the author of Extract A use language to emphasise his views?

SOURCE C

A 1917 Russian illustration showing a woman who has collapsed from hunger while waiting for bread in Petrograd. The signs in the window say 'No bread'.

POLITICAL EFFECTS OF THE FIRST WORLD WAR

The Fourth Duma was suspended in August 1914 to allow the government to concentrate on winning the war. But as the war got worse and worse for Russia, members of the duma demanded that the tsar's failing government should be replaced by duma deputies in a ministry of national confidence. The tsar refused, so around half the duma deputies formed a group called the Progressive Bloc, which became a centre of opposition to the government. When the duma began again in November 1916, it continued to be very critical of the tsarist government and, in particular, the influence of Rasputin.

▶ **Figure 2.1** Impacts of the First World War

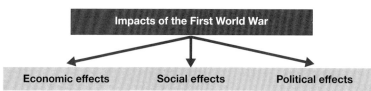

ACTIVITY

Using Figure 2.1, explain one economic effect, one social effect and one political effect of the First World War that made revolution more likely in Russia.

2.2 THE INFLUENCE OF RASPUTIN

LEARNING OBJECTIVES

■ Understand why Tsarina Alexandra became regent

■ Understand the reasons for Alexandra's unpopularity

■ Understand how Rasputin's influence on the royal family increased opposition to tsarist rule.

THE TSARINA IN CONTROL

KEY TERM

regent the person appointed to govern the country because the ruler is away, ill or too young to rule

When Nicholas decided to take on the role of commander-in-chief of Russia's armed forces, he had to go to the army's headquarters, based 800 km from St Petersburg – now known as Petrograd. (When the war started, Russians became strongly anti-German and *Petersburg* sounded Germanic, so the name was changed to the more Russian-sounding *Petrograd*.) Nicholas left his wife Alexandra in Petrograd as his **regent**. This gave her the tsar's power to govern the empire in his absence.

There were three main reasons why, as regent to the empire, the tsarina contributed to the February Revolution in 1917.

■ Alexandra was dedicated to the idea of autocracy as the only way Russia could and should be governed. As a result, she refused to deal with the duma. She used her power to dismiss ministers and replace them with those she preferred. Between August 1915 and December 1916, Alexandra appointed four different prime ministers and three different ministers of war.

■ Alexandra was German, which made her deeply unpopular with the Russian people. Ordinary people often spoke about her in an insulting way.

■ Alexandra became obsessed with a Siberian peasant-monk with mystic healing powers called Grigori Yefimovich Rasputin. Her relationship with Rasputin weakened the authority of the royal family and offended the nobles who considered it their right to give advice to the tsar.

RASPUTIN'S INFLUENCE ON ALEXANDRA

Rasputin both fascinated and shocked people. He believed the best way to connect with God spiritually was by sinning and then **repenting**. To most Russians (who were Orthodox Christians) at the time, sinning meant drinking alcohol, stealing and sex – all three of which Rasputin was accused of doing too much of during his life. Rumours about his exploits made him into a mysterious character.

Prince Alexis – son of the tsar and tsarina, heir to the throne – had been born with the disease haemophilia. This meant his blood did not clot properly, so any kind of injury could be fatal. Doctors could do little to help. Desperately looking for a cure, Tsarina Alexandra turned to spiritual healers. This was how she met Rasputin.

When it seemed that Rasputin was able to help Alexis, Alexandra's gratitude towards the spiritual healer turned into dependence on him. No one in the royal court had closer access to Alexandra than Rasputin. She took his advice, appointed new ministers according to his recommendations, and even wrote to Nicholas telling him about Rasputin's dreams and what they meant the tsar should do next in the war.

OPPOSITION TO RASPUTIN AND ALEXANDRA

Because Rasputin was so influential with the royal family, he was hated by the royal court and those in government. Rasputin also made the royal family look bad. Many cartoons at the time showed him as the real ruler of the Russian empire, with Nicholas and Alexandra as his puppets. Shocking rumours spread that he was having an affair with Alexandra, as well as with

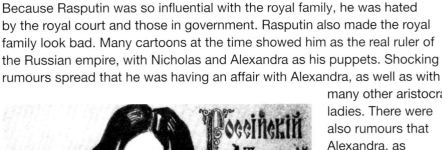

SOURCE D

A Russian cartoon showing Rasputin, the tsar and the tsarina.

EXTEND YOUR KNOWLEDGE

THE MYSTERIES SURROUNDING RASPUTIN'S DEATH
The wild rumours about Rasputin continued after his death. It was said that the aristocrats who set out to murder Rasputin first poisoned him and, when that failed to kill him, shot him. Other rumours were that Rasputin was forced to choose between drinking poison and shooting himself. His body was found trapped under the ice of the Neva River, with injuries suggesting he had been badly beaten before drowning, or that they had happened after death as his body was dragged under the ice. To this day, historians have found it very difficult to be certain about what did happen.

many other aristocratic ladies. There were also rumours that Alexandra, as a German, was deliberately making Russia lose the war by betraying military secrets and sending to Germany the food and guns that Russians so desperately needed.

These rumours were so damaging to the overall image of Russia's ruling class that in December 1916 a group of aristocrats murdered Rasputin. The tsarina was very upset, but in the streets there was public rejoicing.

ACTIVITY

1 Why do you think the cartoonist drew the cartoon in Source D?

2 How far does Source E support the claims made in Source F about Rasputin's influence on the tsar and tsarina?

3 Write a short report on Rasputin's assassination for a newspaper website. Use quotations from Sources E and F to help you. Keep the report to 120 words or fewer.

SOURCE E

From a letter dated 15 November 1915, written by Alexandra to Nicholas giving him advice about fighting the war against Germany.

Now before I forget, I must give you… a message from our Friend [Rasputin] prompted by what He saw in the night. He begs you to order that we should advance near Riga… says it is necessary, otherwise the Germans will settle down so firmly through all the winter, that it will cost endless bloodshed and trouble to make them move… he says this is just now the most essential thing and begs you seriously to order an advance, he says we can and we must, and I was to write it to you at once.

SOURCE F

From a report of 29 December 1916 by Stanlislaus de Lazovert, a Polish aristocrat who had helped to murder Rasputin.

The story of Rasputin and his clique is well known. They sent the army to the trenches without food or arms, they left them there to be slaughtered, they betrayed… and deceived the Allies, they almost succeeded in delivering Russia bodily to the Germans.

Rasputin… had absolute power in Court. The Tsar was a nonentity, … his only desire being to abdicate and escape the whole vile business.

Rasputin continued his life of vice, partying and passion. The Grand Duchess reported these things to the Tsarina and was banished from Court for her pains.

This was the condition of affairs when we decided to kill this monster.

2.3 THE FEBRUARY REVOLUTION, 1917

LEARNING OBJECTIVES

■ Understand the events which led to the February Revolution of 1917

■ Understand the 1917 army mutiny

■ Understand the abdication of the tsar and the setting up of the Provisional Government.

January–February 1917 Mass protests in Petrograd

26 February Troops open fire on demonstrators

1 March Petrograd Soviet issues Order Number 1

23 February 1917 International Women's Day protests

27 February 1917 Army mutinies, Duma Committee set up

2 March 1917 Tsar Nicholas II abdicates and Duma Committee establishes Provisional Government

Although Rasputin was gone, anger continued to grow towards the tsar. The severe winter of 1916–17 led to a shortage of food and fuel. The tsar was away from Petrograd leading the army and was unable to control events in the capital. Opposition to his rule became so severe that, in early 1917, there was a series of revolts against his rule. These revolts were known as the February Revolution. On 2 March, the tsar abdicated and was replaced by a **provisional government**. How had this happened?

LONG-TERM CAUSES OF THE FEBRUARY REVOLUTION

In Chapter 1, you looked at the reasons for discontent in tsarist Russia in 1905. Despite the initial gains made by the middle classes after the 1905 revolution, the same reasons for discontent remained in 1917. The tsar had given up very little of his autocratic powers in practice, and the fear of revolution had made Russia even more of a police state than before. Industrial workers still endured terrible working conditions, many nationalities wanted independence from the rule of the tsar, and the peasants struggled on in conditions of terrible poverty.

IMMEDIATE CAUSES OF THE FEBRUARY REVOLUTION

Discontent with the tsarist government had intensified over the winter of 1916–17. There was despair at the unsuccessful leadership of the Russian armies, now blamed directly on the tsar. Food shortages hit the major cities as railway transport focused on getting supplies out to the front. Peasants also sold less of their grain because there was little to buy with the money they made. Factories had been turned over to war production or had gone out of business due to foreign trade being blocked by Russia's enemies.

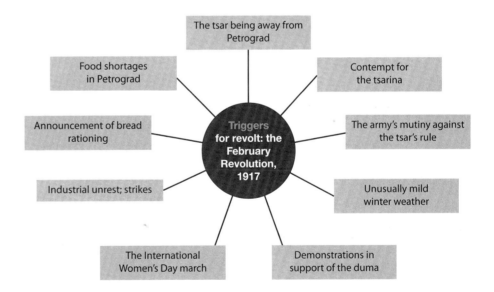

▶ **Figure 2.2** Immediate causes of the February Revolution

On 23 February 1917, International Women's Day, thousands of women marched in protest against bread shortages. They joined the protests led by striking workers. The government announced that bread would have to be rationed in Petrograd, starting on 1 March. The timing of this announcement, which came after a winter of food shortages, was bad; it made people desperate. Between 23 and 25 February, a quarter of a million people then marched through the streets of Petrograd to protest; unusually mild February weather allowed the citizens to gather outside. The number was far more than the police could control. It was the clashes between these demonstrators and the police and army that led to the February Revolution.

Nicholas II had left Petrograd on 22 February to return to army headquarters in Mogilev, so he was not in the capital to take charge of the situation. His regent in Petrograd, Tsarina Alexandra, was mistrusted as a German; she was hated and ridiculed. Nicholas had to rely on reports sent to him as the revolution developed. On 25 February, he ordered the police and soldiers to enter Petrograd to end the unrest. The next day, some soldiers opened fire on protesters, killing more than 50 people. This was a crucial turning point both for the protesters, who called this a second Bloody Sunday, and for the soldiers, who were now forced to make a decision: should they defend the regime against its people, or join the people against the tsar, their supreme leader?

SOURCE G

A demonstration of the Putilov Steelworkers at the start of the February Revolution. The banners read: 'Increase rations to the families of soldiers – the defenders of freedom and world peace' and 'Feed the children of the defenders of the Motherland'.

EXAM-STYLE QUESTION

A01

Describe **two** features of the social impacts of the First World War in Russia.

(6 marks)

HINT

Remember to support each of the two features you write about with accurate detail.

THE ARMY MUTINY

On 26 February, soldiers of the Pavlovsky Regiment learned about the shooting of more than 50 people by trainee soldiers from another Petrograd regiment. The Pavlovsky soldiers were shocked that Russian soldiers were shooting Russian citizens. They refused to obey orders to fire on demonstrators. This was a mutiny, a **rebellion** by soldiers against the orders of their officers. Over the next 2 days (27–28 February), soldiers joined with workers to capture Petrograd's main weapons store; they took over 40,000 rifles and 30,000 revolvers. They also broke into prisons and released political prisoners.

Not all the soldiers mutinied, but those who did came from several different regiments, including new troops sent into the city from outside Petrograd. With the involvement of soldiers, the revolution had now properly begun. Workers and soldiers joined together as police stations were attacked, while running battles were taking place in the streets against the police forces.

SOURCE H

A postcard from February 1917 showing a mounted soldier slashing at a policeman, who is shown firing his pistol into the crowd. The red banner in the picture reads 'Bread'. In the background there is a monument to the unpopular, anti-reform Tsar Alexander III: a symbol of tsarist autocracy. The statue was destroyed with dynamite in March 1917.

The number of soldiers who mutinied and joined the protests reached 150,000, which was almost the whole military defence force for the city of Petrograd. The mutiny made the fall of the tsar almost certain, because without the soldiers' support, Nicholas' government had no real way of controlling the city. The police force in Petrograd was not big enough to fight 150,000 mutinous soldiers and 250,000 demonstrators. Soldiers in other parts of Russia could be called to Petrograd to restore order, but most were so tired of the First World War that their army commanders were almost certain they too would join the protests if they had the chance.

SOURCE I

From a letter written in spring 1917 by Feodor Linde, a sergeant in the Finland Regiment in Petrograd, describing his involvement in the army mutiny. The Cossacks were the army's elite mounted troops, who were fiercely loyal to the tsar.

The Cossacks were firing on defenceless and unarmed crowds, striking people with their whips, crushing the fallen with their horses. And then I saw a young girl trying to evade the galloping horse of a Cossack officer. She was too slow. A severe blow on her head brought her down under the horse's feet. She screamed. It was her inhuman, penetrating scream that caused something in me to snap. I jumped to the table and cried out wildly: 'Friends! Friends! Long live the revolution! To arms! To arms! They are killing innocent people, our brothers and sisters!' … They [the other soldiers] all joined me in the attack against the Cossacks and police. We killed a few. The rest retreated… The revolution had become a reality.

SOURCE J

From the memoirs of A. P. Balk, governor of Petrograd in February 1917, written in 1929.

February 25 was a total defeat for us. Not only were the leaders of the revolutionary action convinced that the troops were acting without spirit, even unwillingly, but the crowd also sensed the weakness of the authorities and became emboldened. The decision of the military authorities to impose control by force, in exceptional circumstances to use arms, not only poured oil on the fire but shook up the troops and allowed them to think that the authorities… feared 'the people'.

EXAM-STYLE QUESTION

A03

SKILLS   ANALYSIS, ADAPTIVE LEARNING, CREATIVITY

Study Sources I and J.
How far does Source I support the evidence of Source J about the role of the army in the February Revolution?
Explain your answer.   **(8 marks)**

HINT

Plan your answer first by quickly listing the points made in Source I and in Source J. Which points agree with each other? Which points do not?

THE ABDICATION OF THE TSAR

When Nicholas II received reports of the mutiny in Petrograd on 27 February, he ordered General Nikolay Iudovich Ivanov to take troops to the capital and enforce order. The tsar also decided to travel to Petrograd himself, against the advice of his staff. By 1 March, he had reached the city of Pskov. The plan to take back control of Petrograd did not go well. Some of Ivanov's troops began to show signs of mutiny. The army leaders were worried that bringing more troops to Petrograd would only create a larger mutiny, perhaps even a revolution throughout Russia – then Russia would definitely not be able to keep fighting the war.

EXTEND YOUR KNOWLEDGE

DATES FOR REVOLUTIONARY RUSSIA

Before February 1918, Russia used a different calendar from the one used in the West. The Russian calendar is known as Old-Style, or Julian, calendar; it was 13 days behind the calendar used in the West (which is known as New-Style, or Gregorian, calendar; it is what we use today). Historians tend to use Old-Style dates for Russian revolutionary history, sometimes adding 'OS' or 'NS' (for Old Style and New Style) to make it clear which calendar they are using. Under the New-Style system, the February Revolution would therefore be called the March Revolution.

EXTRACT B

From a history of Russia, published in 1960.

The collapse of the Romanov autocracy in March 1917 was one of the most leaderless, spontaneous, anonymous revolutions of all time.

ACTIVITY

What impression do you think the author of Extract B is trying to create when he calls the March 1917 revolution 'leaderless, spontaneous, anonymous'?

On 2 March, senior army officers and members of the duma came to Pskov. They urged Nicholas to abdicate in order to save Russia from destruction. Nicholas could see there was no alternative. He agreed to abdicate in favour of his brother, Grand Duke Michael.

The reaction in Petrograd to the possibility of a new tsar was very negative, however. The revolutionaries wanted a complete end to autocracy. The leaders of the Provisional Government warned Michael that, if he did accept, the revolution would turn into a civil war. Michael was not keen to be tsar in the first place, and did not take much persuading to turn down his brother's offer.

After 300 years of Romanov rule, Russia became a republic in spring 1917.

SOURCE K

The front page of the *Daily Sketch*, a British tabloid, on the day after the announcement of the tsar's abdication: this was 16 March in the UK as Russia still used a calendar that was 13 days behind.

ACTIVITY

Put together your own contemporary newspaper front page describing the events of the February Revolution up to the abdication of the tsar. Your front page could include:

- ■ a suitable photo
- ■ a timeline of events
- ■ reasons for the revolution and analysis of possible consequences.

THE SETTING UP OF THE PROVISIONAL GOVERNMENT

The revolution on the streets caused a power vacuum. On the one hand, the St Petersburg Soviet of Workers' Delegates (which originally emerged during the 1905 revolutions) re-formed to become the Petrograd Soviet of Workers' and Soldiers' Deputies, after huge numbers of soldiers declared their support for the revolution and the soviet decided to represent both workers and soldiers. On the other hand, 12 duma representatives set up a provisional committee, after a request to the tsar to let the duma share power was refused.

On 2 March 1917, as soon as Nicholas II abdicated and his brother Michael had turned down the throne, the Provisional Government was formed, with a well-known liberal, Prince Lvov, as its leader. The idea was that the Provisional Government would run Russia until democratic elections could take place for a Constituent Assembly: these were expected to be held within 6 months. As the Provisional Government took over, police authorities as well as local town and countryside councils across Russia collapsed. This was a major problem for the new government, as they needed to rule the country through these local structures. At the same time, Russia was still at war. So, on 3 March, the Provisional Government issued a manifesto. It set out the eight principles of government as follows:

1 political prisoners and exiles to be freed from prison or allowed to return to Russia
2 freedom of speech, freedom of the press and freedom to hold meetings
3 no class, religious or nationality **discrimination**
4 preparations to be started for electing a Constituent Assembly to write a constitution
5 all police organisations to be replaced by an elected people's militia
6 local governments to be elected
7 military units that took part in the revolution should not be disbanded or sent to the front to fight
8 off-duty soldiers to have the same rights as civilians.

ACTIVITY

1 Which of the eight principles do you think were influenced by the Petrograd Soviet of Workers' and Soldiers' Deputies? Explain your answer.
2 Which of the reasons for discontent with tsarism listed in Chapter 1 (see page 5) are reflected in the eight principles? Which ones are not?
3 'The February Revolution was a riot over food shortages, not the planned political overthrow of tsarism.' How far would you agree with this interpretation?

ACTIVITY

Explain in your own words what the writers of Source L were referring to by the following phrases:

■ 'the old order has been overthrown'
■ 'All attempts to bring the Government to its senses proved futile'
■ 'the Government [was] in a state of moral decay'
■ 'Russia… was confronted with gravest disasters'
■ 'free civic organisation' (civic means people's responsibilities for looking after their local area and country)

SOURCE M

A postcard from 1917 showing Prince Lvov, leader of the Provisional Government. The text underneath his portrait reads 'Free Russia'. Prince Lvov was used to dealing with **zemstvo** governments and found working with different political parties very difficult.

KEY TERM

zemstvo Russian local government. There were *zemstvos* for rural areas and for towns. They were mainly run by local liberal gentry

SOURCE L

From the Provisional Government's manifesto of 3 March 1917.

Citizens of Russia:

A great event has taken place. By the mighty assault of the Russian people, the old order has been overthrown. A new, free Russia is born. The great revolution crowns long years of struggle…

All attempts to bring the Government to its senses proved futile, and the titanic world struggle, into which the country was dragged by the enemy, found the Government in a state of moral decay, alienated from the people, indifferent to the fate of our native land, and [full of] corruption… And when Russia, owing to the illegal and fatal actions of her rulers, was confronted with gravest disasters, the nation was obliged to take the power into its own hands.

The unanimous revolutionary enthusiasm of the people… and the determination of the State Duma, have created the Provisional Government, which considers it to be its sacred and responsible duty to fulfil the hopes of the nation, and lead the country out onto the bright path of free civic organization.

RECAP

RECALL QUESTIONS

1 Name two countries Russia fought against in the First World War.
2 What happened between 26 and 30 August 1914 at Tannenburg, during the first month of the First World War?
3 What did Nicholas II decide to do in August 1915, against the advice of military and government advisers?
4 Grigori Yefimovich was a Siberian peasant-monk with mystic healing powers. What other name did he have?
5 The February Revolution is thought to have begun with marches on International Women's Day. Which Old-Style date did this happen on?
6 Approximately how many soldiers joined the February Revolution in Petrograd following the army mutiny?
7 On 2 March 1917, senior army leaders and duma representatives travelled to a railway carriage in Pskov to do what?
8 Who did Nicholas name to be tsar in his place?
9 Who was the first leader of the Provisional Government?
10 Why was the Provisional Government called 'provisional'?

CHECKPOINT

STRENGTHEN

S1 Identify two similarities between the 1905 revolution and the February Revolution.
S2 Identify two differences between the 1905 revolution and the February Revolution.
S3 Explain three triggers (short-term causes) of the February Revolution.

CHALLENGE

C1 If Russia had not entered the First World War, do you think tsarism would have survived? Give at least two reasons for your answer.
C2 Explain the problems facing Nicholas II at the start of 1917.
C3 What one thing do you think the tsar could have done to prevent himself from being forced to abdicate? Why do you think he didn't do it?

SUMMARY

- In 1914, Russia went to war on the side of France and Britain.
- Early defeats in the war led to the tsar becoming more unpopular.
- In 1915, the tsar appointed himself commander-in-chief of the Russian forces.
- The war caused shortages and hardships in Russia.
- While the tsar was away fighting, the tsarina came under the influence of Rasputin.
- A severe winter in 1916/17 caused food shortages and led to increased discontent.
- In February 1917, 150,000 soldiers mutinied.
- The Petrograd Soviet became increasingly important.
- In March 1917, the tsar abdicated.
- After the tsar's abdication, the Provisional Government set out to govern Russia, saying it would do so only until democratic elections were held.

EXAM GUIDANCE: PART (B) QUESTIONS

Study Sources A and B.

SOURCE A

From a letter dated 15 November 1915, written by Alexandra to Nicholas giving him advice about fighting the war against Germany.

Now before I forget, I must give you… a message from our Friend [Rasputin] prompted by what He saw in the night. He begs you to order that we should advance near Riga… says it is necessary, otherwise the Germans will settle down so firmly through all the winter, that it will cost endless bloodshed and trouble to make them move… he says this is just now the most essential thing and begs you seriously to order an advance, he says we can and we must, and I was to write it to you at once.

SOURCE B

From a report of 29 December 1916 by Stanlislaus de Lazovert, a Polish aristocrat who had helped to murder Rasputin.

The story of Rasputin and his clique is well known. They sent the army to the trenches without food or arms, they left them there to be slaughtered, they betrayed… and deceived the Allies, they almost succeeded in delivering Russia bodily to the Germans.

Rasputin… had absolute power in Court. The Tsar was a nonentity, … his only desire being to abdicate and escape the whole vile business.

Rasputin continued his life of vice, partying and passion. The Grand Duchess reported these things to the Tsarina and was banished from Court for her pains.

This was the condition of affairs when we decided to kill this monster.

AO3

SKILLS ANALYSIS, ADAPTIVE LEARNING, CREATIVITY

Question to be answered: How far does Source A support the evidence of Source B about Rasputin's influence in Russia?

Explain your answer.   **(8 marks)**

1 **Analysis Question 1: What is the question type testing?**
In this question, you have to demonstrate that you can comprehend, interpret and cross-refer sources. In this question, that means you can see similarities and differences between the two sources in what they say about the influence Rasputin had.

2 **Analysis Question 2: What do I have to do to answer the question well?**
You have to write about points and areas of agreement and difference between the two sources that you are given. Do not be tempted to tell the examiner what each source says. The examiner will already know that! Go straight for the agreements and differences. You might, for example, say, 'The main areas of agreement between the two sources are…' or 'The sources both agree that…' or 'The two sources differ about…'.

3 **Analysis Question 3: Are there any techniques I can use to make it very clear that I am doing what is needed to be successful?**
This is an 8-mark question, and you need to be sure you leave enough time to answer the part (c) question, which is worth 16 marks. So you need to get straight in to your answer. Divide it into three parts. In the first paragraph, identify areas and points of agreement; in the second paragraph, do the same but identify differences. Remember to quote from the source material to support what you are saying. Your final paragraph should explain the extent of the support or agreement between the two sources – that is, how strongly they agree or disagree.

You must identify both agreement and difference. You will get up to 5 marks for doing this, and for supporting what you have selected with material from the sources. (You can only receive a maximum of 4 marks if you do 'just one side'.) There are 3 additional marks for explaining the extent to which one source supports the other.

Answer

The sources agree that Rasputin was very influential. Source A tells us that Rasputin had such an influence over the Tsarina that she wrote to her husband and told him to lead an advance because he had a dream about it and thought it was a good idea. He is nowhere near the front, but still he is thought to be someone who could advise on military tactics. Source B also shows how Rasputin had a lot of influence because he is described as having absolute power. When the Grand Duchess complained, she was banished from court.

But Source B also fails to support Source A. The impression given in Source A is that Rasputin is popular (he is called 'our friend') and there is no suggestion of opposition. But in Source B there is criticism of the way he nearly lost Russia to the Germans. There is obviously complaint (from people like the Grand Duchess) and they killed him!

What are the strengths of this answer?

- *The support and lack of support between the sources is clearly identified in separate paragraphs.*
- *The points made in each paragraph are supported by appropriate quotations from the sources.*

What are the weaknesses?

- *There is no conclusion explaining how far the sources support each other. Although support and lack of support is shown, there is no attempt to assess the strength or extent of the support.*

Answer checklist

☐ Identifies support
☐ Identifies lack of support
☐ Provides information from the sources to support the statements
☐ Considers the extent of the support/disagreement – which is stronger?

3. PROVISIONAL GOVERNMENT AND THE BOLSHEVIK REVOLUTION

LEARNING OBJECTIVES

- Understand the weaknesses and mistakes of the Provisional Government
- Understand the reasons for the support won by Lenin and the Bolsheviks
- Understand the events of the Bolshevik takeover.

The Provisional Government faced enormous challenges, and its ability to deal effectively with these challenges was seriously reduced by the weakness of its position and the mistakes it made. One significant weakness involved the Petrograd Soviet, which shared the government of Russia in a system known as Dual Control, thus weakening the authority of the Provisional Government. One significant mistake was the determination of the Provisional Government to continue Russian involvement in the First World War. The unpopularity of the war increased following the failure of Russia's June Offensive in 1917.

As support for the Provisional Government decreased throughout 1917, support for the Bolsheviks increased. Lenin's key demands (as set out in his April Theses) – 'Peace, Land and Bread' and 'All Power to the Soviets!' – connected with the suffering population of Petrograd as well as the peasants, who were desperate for more land. By October 1917, Lenin believed the time was right for the Bolshevik Party to seize power in the name of the soviets.

3.1 WEAKNESSES AND MISTAKES OF THE PROVISIONAL GOVERNMENT

LEARNING OBJECTIVES

- Understand the challenges facing the Provisional Government
- Understand the weaknesses and mistakes of the Provisional Government
- Understand how the Petrograd Soviet weakened the authority of the Provisional Government.

WEAKNESSES OF THE PROVISIONAL GOVERNMENT

The principal weakness of the Provisional Government was that it shared power with the Petrograd Soviet. Historians have called this Dual Control: both the Provisional Government and the Petrograd Soviet had some power, but neither was in full control of the country.

The main challenges faced by the Provisional Government were as follows.

- The 'Dual Control' meant there were key areas of government that the Provisional Government had no control over because it answered to the Petrograd Soviet, for example, the railway system and the post service. This made it very difficult for the government to increase transportation of food to the cities, for example.
- The Petrograd Soviet had a rule called 'Order Number 1', which meant that it, not the Provisional Government, had the final say on military matters. This damaged the authority of the Provisional Government. A government could not work effectively if its orders were only followed if another organisation gave its permission.
- The Petrograd Soviet was elected, but no one had elected the Provisional Government. It was made up of deputies who had been elected to the duma, but that had happened under tsarism. As it had not been elected by the people it was supposed to govern, this weakened the authority of the Provisional Government.

ACTIVITY

Imagine that, in your school, teachers were only allowed to give detentions if the school council said it was fine.
- Why might teachers find that difficult?
- How is this scenario linked to one of the weaknesses of the Provisional Government?

SOURCE A

From 'Order Number 1', published by the Petrograd garrison and then by the Petrograd Soviet.

1. *In all companies, battalions, regiments… and on the vessels of the navy, committees of elected representatives shall be chosen… from the lower ranks of the above-mentioned military units.*

2. *The orders of the military commission of the State duma shall be executed only in such cases as they do not conflict with the orders and resolutions of the Soviet of Workers' and Soldiers' Deputies [the Petrograd Soviet].*

SOURCE B

The Leader of the government, Prince Lvov (in the centre). The man to the right of Prince Lvov is Alexander Kerensky, minister of war.

MISTAKES OF THE PROVISIONAL GOVERNMENT

In addition to its weaknesses, the Provisional Government also made a number of mistakes once it was set up.

- Continuing the First World War: The Provisional Government was desperate to continue the war, as it was relying on other Allied countries to invest in Russia's recovery; if Russia pulled out of the war, the other countries might turn away from Russia. This proved to be a mistake, as most ordinary people wanted Russia out of the war as soon as possible.

- Delaying elections: The Provisional Government always intended to call elections to the Constituent Assembly, but it found a general election to be very difficult to organise, and there were also many other serious problems needing attention. But by delaying the elections, the Provisional Government looked as though it was trying to stay in power without being elected.

- Delaying reforms: The peasants wanted more land, taken from the landlords. The Provisional Government did not act on this, believing that whatever land reform was carried out should be decided by the Constituent Assembly. It was also true that the Provisional Government only had control over the cities and towns in the north of Russia; it had little authority elsewhere.

- Allowing more freedom: One step which the Provisional Government took was to introduce greater freedom of speech. It was now legal to hold meetings and set up political parties. While this may have reduced the autocracy of the tsar's rule, it also allowed people to openly criticise the Provisional Government.

THE JUNE OFFENSIVE

In May 1917, Alexander Kerensky was appointed minister of war. In June, Kerensky decided that the Russian army should launch a major offensive: an attack on enemy positions. It was believed that a victory against the Austrians and Germans would win support for the Provisional Government and help boost army confidence, which had been very low in the Russian army. Unfortunately, the June Offensive was a disaster. The Russian front collapsed and the Russian army was pushed back hundreds of kilometres. The June Offensive showed that the Russian military could not rely on its soldiers to follow orders.

KEY TERM

legitimacy the quality of being acceptable or allowed by law

ACTIVITY

Figure 3.1 shows the weaknesses and mistakes of the Provisional Government. Study the diagram, choose three points and explain them to a partner, before asking your partner to choose and explain three points. Then, go over the remaining three points and make sure you both understand what they mean.

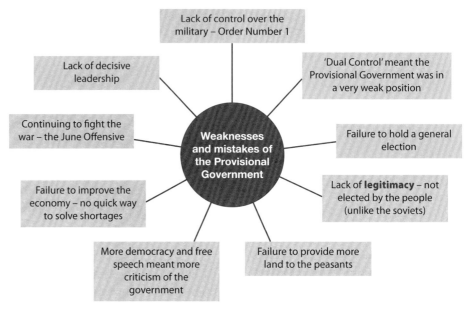

▲ **Figure 3.1** Weaknesses and mistakes of the Provisional Government

THE IMPACT OF THE PETROGRAD SOVIET

The Petrograd Soviet was set up after the Mensheviks (minority members of the Russian Social Democratic Party) encouraged workers to form a soviet like the one set up in 1905. At first, it represented factory workers, but soon it was dominated by soldiers. The sessions of the soviet could have as many as 3,000 people in them, sometimes with many people talking at once. So it was difficult to reach an agreed decision. In any case, it was the Petrograd Soviet's **executive committee** that made most of the actual decisions.

Because it was elected and respected by ordinary Russians, the Petrograd Soviet could potentially have pushed the Provisional Government aside and made an attempt to govern Russia on its own. However, despite having passed Order Number 1, the soviet did not really challenge the Provisional Government between March and April of 1917. The soviet's impact on Russia was limited because of the following factors.

■ Both the Petrograd Soviet and the Provisional Government were very worried about tsarist forces trying to take back control of Russia. The soviet therefore did not want to weaken the Provisional Government.

■ The Petrograd Soviet was run by Mensheviks and other Marxists, who wanted a socialist revolution for Russia. However, they believed that there had to be a **bourgeois** phase in Russia before there could be a socialist revolution. The Provisional Government was a bourgeois government, which was why the soviet supported it.

KEY TERM

bourgeois belonging to or typical of the part of society that is rich, educated, owns land, etc.

SOURCE C

From a speech made by a Menshevik in the summer of 1917.

The provisional government possesses no real power and its orders are executed only in so far as this is permitted by the Soviet Workers' and Soldiers' Deputies, which holds in its hands the most important elements of actual power, such as troops, railroads, postal and telegraph service...

■ Russia already had many problems to deal with; the Petrograd Soviet kept itself out of the duma because it did not want to start getting blamed for all the things going wrong in Russia.

Instead of challenging the Provisional Government directly, the Petrograd Soviet aimed to use its power to influence government policies and make sure they were in the interests of ordinary people and soldiers. Many of the principles of government set out on 3 March 1917 by the Provisional Government (see page 38) were things that the Soviet had demanded the government do: for example, freedom for political prisoners and the abolition of the police.

The Petrograd Soviet's Order Number 1 was also a major problem for the Provisional Government. Since soldiers would only carry out the orders of the government if the Soviet approved them, the government had no real control. This would have been difficult in peacetime, but the Provisional Government was in charge of a country at war – a war that the Government had promised to continue.

Although Mensheviks did not believe Russian workers were ready to take control from the Provisional Government, Lenin was convinced that the time was right for his Bolshevik Party to seize power and create a workers' state. As support for the Bolsheviks increased through 1917, Lenin worked to get control of the Petrograd Soviet Executive so he could use it to seize control of Russia. By September, he had achieved his goal. A majority of the Soviet delegates were Bolshevik supporters. This was very important for the October revolution of 1917.

SOURCE D

From a resolution passed by the All-Russian Congress of Soviets of Workers' and Soldiers Deputies in June 1917.

[The Congress] agrees that:

1. *...It would have been a severe blow to the revolution to have handed over power to the bourgeoisie [the Provisional Government] alone; and*

2. *That it would have greatly weakened and threatened the revolution to have handed over all the power, at this time, to the Soviets of Workers' and Soldiers' Deputies, for such an act would have alienated certain elements of the population, who are still able to serve the cause of the revolution...*

Therefore the Congress calls on the revolutionary democracy of Russia to gather around the Soviets and to support the Provisional Government energetically...

EXAM-STYLE QUESTION

A03

SKILLS ANALYSIS, ADAPTIVE LEARNING, CREATIVITY

Study Sources C and D.
How far does Source C support the evidence of Source D about the relationship between the Provisional Government and the Petrograd Soviet? Explain your answer.   **(8 marks)**

HINT

Make sure you include both ways in which the two sources agree, and ways in which they disagree.

3.2 THE ACTIVITIES OF LENIN AND THE BOLSHEVIKS

LEARNING OBJECTIVES

■ Understand the activities of Lenin and the Bolsheviks in 1917

■ Understand the changes Lenin argued for in his April Theses

■ Understand the events of the July Days.

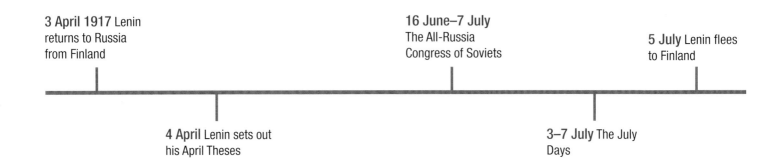

3 April 1917 Lenin returns to Russia from Finland

16 June–7 July The All-Russia Congress of Soviets

5 July Lenin flees to Finland

4 April Lenin sets out his April Theses

3–7 July The July Days

LENIN RETURNS TO RUSSIA

By 1917, Lenin had already been in exile from Russia for 10 years. He knew about the February Revolution only through reports sent to him in Switzerland. He was desperate to return to Russia, but it took a long time to convince the Germans to let him cross their territory on his way back from Switzerland. Although the Germans were keen to have Lenin back in Russia, arguing for an end to their enemy Russia's involvement in the First World War, they were also worried about Lenin encouraging revolution in Germany. Lenin was finally permitted to travel, but he was put on a train that was sealed closed to stop him interacting with German socialists as he travelled through Germany.

At this time, the Bolsheviks were not in a strong position. Leading Bolsheviks like Kamenev and Stalin agreed with the Mensheviks that Russia was a long way from a socialist revolution and the main thing now was to defend the February Revolution from counter-revolution. They made speeches to **campaign** for more **followers**, and helped workers organise strikes.

When Lenin arrived at the Finland Station in Petrograd on 3 April 1917, he was met by a crowd of supporters. He climbed onto the top of an armoured car and said:

ACTIVITY

Explain what Lenin is criticising the Provisional Government for in his Finland Station speech.

I greet you without knowing yet whether or not you have believed in all the promises of the Provisional Government. But I am convinced that when they talk to you sweetly, when they promise you a lot, they are deceiving you and the whole Russian people. The people need peace; the people need bread; the people need land. And they give you war, hunger, no bread – leave the landlords still on the land... We must fight for the social revolution, fight to the end, until the complete victory of the proletariat. Long live the worldwide socialist revolution!

THE APRIL THESES

Lenin was a devoted follower of Karl Marx, and his ambition was to bring a Marxist revolution to Russia. While others were happy to spend time discussing the theory of Marxism, Lenin wanted to see it happen. The Bolsheviks had thought that they needed to wait until Russia was fully capitalist, with a huge proletariat population like in England or Germany before launching a revolution. Lenin thought differently. On his journey back to Russia, Lenin wrote the April Theses, which set out his views on what the Bolsheviks should do.

In the April Theses, Lenin proposed the following:

- ending all co-operation with the Provisional Government and with any other party that was helping the Provisional Government (including the Mensheviks and the Socialist Revolutionary Party)
- a campaign to end the war; it was a war between capitalists that had nothing to offer the proletariat except death and suffering
- the nationalisation of all land; the landlords' estates would all be taken away and given to peasants
- educating workers and peasants so they could see that all power must go to the soviets; the soviets must then take over state power from the Provisional Government, and abolish the police, the army and **bureaucracy**
- industry should be controlled by the soviets, with all banks combining into one state bank.

Lenin's arguments boiled down to two simple slogans: '*Peace, Land and Bread*' and '*All Power to the Soviets!*'.

KEY TERM

bureaucracy the officials who are employed (rather than elected) to do government work

SOURCE E

Lenin speaking at the All-Russia Conference of Soviets of Workers' and Soldiers' Deputies on 4 April 1917.

ACTIVITY

Write a speech that expresses Lenin's view about socialist revolution in Russia. It should explain why the slogans 'Peace, Land and Bread' and 'All Power to the Soviets!' were important. Who would be likely to support each of the two slogans?

GROWING SUPPORT FOR THE BOLSHEVIKS

Lenin's strong personality and absolute determination convinced other Bolsheviks to follow his lead. The Bolsheviks promoted Lenin's simple, powerful slogans to the Petrograd workers. But the Bolshevik Party was still very small in April 1917. The Socialist Revolutionary Party (SRs) had far more support than the Bolsheviks, especially among the peasants – the vast majority of the population. The Mensheviks were more popular than the Bolsheviks among many of the workers in Russia's industrial cities. The soviets were not Bolshevik organisations. In June 1917, a meeting known as the All-Russian Congress of Soviets was organised to bring together representatives from all the soviets in Russia. Only 13 per cent of the representatives were Bolsheviks, compared with 66 per cent from the SRs and Mensheviks.

However, support for the Bolsheviks grew through the summer of 1917. This was partly because of Lenin's strong leadership and Trotsky's excellent organisation, but also because of the Provisional Government's continuing weaknesses (as mentioned on page 44).
- By June 1917, Bolshevik newspapers appeared in most of Russia's industrial cities, all strongly criticising the Provisional Government.
- Lenin's April Theses provided a clear, strong message for the Bolsheviks to take into the factories, navy and army. They explained how the party would end the war and give state power to the soviets; how it would govern the country for ordinary workers, not for the wealthy.
- The Bolsheviks were successful in recruiting armed workers' **militias**, called the Red Guards, to the party. By July there were around 10,000 Red Guards in Petrograd, most of them loyal to the Bolsheviks.
- Germany secretly sent the Bolsheviks money to pay for their activities – the Germans hoped Lenin would succeed in persuading Russians to pull out of the war.

Lenin said that the Bolsheviks were ready to seize power from the Provisional Government. However, he always explained that in time the Bolsheviks would do this for the proletariat and that, following his slogan 'All Power to the Soviets!', the Bolsheviks would then hand over the state to the soviets to run. Workers supported the Bolsheviks because they believed that the party would help them to take control of the factories for themselves.

KEY TERM

militia civilians who fight alongside the army

THE JULY DAYS

In March 1917, the Provisional Government introduced bread rationing; in the following months, the amount of bread available declined. Meanwhile, the war was continuing to use up vital food and fuel. In June, the Provisional Government launched a major offensive against Austrian and German forces. The government had hoped a victory would win some support and help boost army morale, which was very low. Unfortunately, the June Offensive was a

EXTRACT A

From a history of Russia, published in 1966.

The July Days had a catastrophic effect on the Bolshevik Party. On the night of 4–5 July, the Government published documents, partly forged, saying that Lenin was a German agent. Anti-Bolshevik feelings spread through wide areas of the country.

ACTIVITY

What impression does Extract A give you of the Provisional Government?

KEY TERM

anarchist someone who believes that governments, laws, etc. are not necessary

disaster. The Russian front collapsed and the Russian army was pushed back hundreds of kilometres. The June Offensive showed that the Russian military could not rely on their soldiers to follow orders. It is estimated that by October 1917, over 2 million soldiers had deserted.

Between 3 and 7 July 1917, an uprising known as the July Days took place. There were three main reasons for the uprising:

- the continuing shortages of food in the major cities
- the complete failure of the June Offensive
- effective Bolshevik **propaganda** against the Provisional Government.

The uprising was started by **anarchist** revolutionaries, who convinced soldiers to join an anti-government demonstration. The Bolsheviks had initially tried to prevent the demonstration, but then decided the time had come to act and began to call on their supporters to join in. Lenin had the idea that the Provisional Government could be overthrown in just the same way that the February Revolution ended tsarism. Tens of thousands of workers and soldiers marched with banners calling for power to be handed to the soviets.

However, the Petrograd Soviet did not support the demonstration; other parties in the soviet did not trust the Bolsheviks. The soviet leadership met with the leaders of the Provisional Government and agreed to work together. A thunderstorm on 4 July dispersed the crowds. On 5 July, the government brought troops back from the front and asked them to surround Bolshevik headquarters. Hundreds of Bolsheviks were arrested, including Trotsky. Lenin escaped and fled to Finland; his plans to overthrow the Provisional Government lay in ruins.

SOURCE F

A photograph of the July Days. It shows government troops firing on demonstrators.

ACTIVITY

Write a letter as Lenin to the remaining Bolshevik supporters in Petrograd explaining where you think things went wrong with the July Days. Set out your argument as a list.

THE KORNILOV REVOLT

Alexander Kerensky had taken a lot of the credit for putting down the July Days uprising; he accused members of the Bolshevik leadership of being German spies. Kerensky subsequently became leader of the Provisional Government.

To tackle the problems of the war, the economy and opposition from the Bolsheviks, Kerensky planned to restore discipline in the army to help prevent defeat in the war: a disciplined army could also then be used to restore order in Russia's cities. He knew this approach would increase support for himself and support for the Provisional Government from Russia's conservatives if it succeeded. To do this, on 18 July 1917 Kerensky appointed a new commander-in-chief for the Russian army. The new commander's name was General Kornilov. The two agreed to bring troops to Petrograd to use in case of unrest.

Unfortunately for Kerensky, Kornilov was not an easy man to control. He wanted Kerensky to introduce martial law and break the power of the soviets. Many of Russia's middle-class people strongly supported this idea because they were worried about the workers seizing their homes, businesses and belongings. Kerensky, however, saw this as a challenge to his leadership and dismissed Kornilov as commander-in-chief. Despite this, Kornilov sent troops to Petrograd on 24 August, with a plan of shutting down the Petrograd Soviet and restoring order in the city.

SOURCE G

From a speech by General Kornilov, reported in a Petrograd newspaper in August 1917.

People of Russia, our great country is dying. Her end is near.

Forced to speak openly, I, General Kornilov, declare that the Provisional Government, under the pressure of the Bolshevik majority in the Soviets, … is killing the army and shaking the country.

The terrible conviction of the inevitable ruin of the country compels me in these frightful times to call upon all Russians to save their dying land…

I, General Kornilov, son of a Cossack peasant, declare to one and all that I desire nothing for myself other than the salvation of our Great Russia, and vow to lead the people, through victory over our enemies, to the Constituent Assembly, where it can determine its future destiny and the form of its future political life.

I cannot betray Russia into the hands of her ancient enemy, the Germans, who would make slaves of the Russian people.

ACTIVITY

1 Using Source G, explain in your own words who General Kornilov blamed for the threats to Russia.
2 Explain why Kornilov thought the Provisional Government was being influenced by the Petrograd Soviet and the Bolsheviks.
3 Would this speech have encouraged Kerensky to think that Kornilov was acting for the Provisional Government or against it? Explain your answer.

There was huge alarm in Petrograd among all the citizens who supported the revolution. Soldiers and workers began preparing to defend the city. Kerensky feared that Kornilov was going to take power for the military. So, as Kornilov approached Petrograd, Kerensky allowed the Bolsheviks to arm their supporters so they could defend the city and the Petrograd Soviet from Kornilov. The Bolsheviks took charge of preparing defences in the city, using armed Red Guard units. At the same time, railway workers blocked Kornilov's route into Petrograd. The Bolsheviks convinced Kornilov's troops to stop their march and desert their officers. Kornilov was arrested on 1 September.

SOURCE H

The meeting of the Red Guards and Kornilov's troops in August 1917.

EXAM-STYLE QUESTION

A01

Describe **two** features of the Kornilov Revolt (August 1917). **(6 marks)**

HINT

Support your identification of a feature with details from your knowledge.

IMPACT OF THE KORNILOV REVOLT

The Kornilov Revolt is often seen as a crucial turning point in the Russian Revolution because it boosted support for the Bolsheviks while weakening Kerensky and the Provisional Government. The event made Kerensky look very weak because he had to rely on the Bolsheviks to defend Petrograd and his government. The Provisional Government lost crucial support.

The Bolsheviks were able to present themselves as having saved Petrograd; they were the defenders of the revolution. Many more Bolsheviks were elected to the soviets and they soon had control of the Petrograd Soviet. On 25 September, Trotsky was elected president of the soviet. At the start of 1917, the Bolshevik Party had 24,000 members. By October 1917, they had 340,000 members, including 60,000 in Petrograd.

The Red Guards added military power to the Bolsheviks: 40,000 Bolshevik supporters kept hold of their weapons after the Kornilov Revolt had ended. Army discipline collapsed as officers were accused of being part of the counter-revolution. Hundreds of them were murdered. Tens of thousands of soldiers deserted and returned to their villages. Incidents of peasants rioting and seizing land increased across the Russian countryside.

SOURCE I

From a speech by Lenin to the Central Committee of the Bolshevik Party, 30 August 1917.

The Kornilov revolt is a most unexpected and downright unbelievably sharp turn in events... Even now we must not support Kerensky's government... We may be asked: aren't we going to fight against Kornilov? Of course we must! ... We shall fight, we are fighting against Kornilov, just as Kerensky's troops do, but we do not support Kerensky. On the contrary, we expose his weakness. There is the difference.

EXTRACT B

From an interview with a historian in 2017.

The Kornilov crisis was an extremely important moment in the events of 1917. The Bolsheviks had been saying that there would be no genuine reform, nor an end to the war by trying to work peacefully with the governing bourgeoisie. This crisis seemed to prove that they were right and support for the Bolsheviks increased dramatically, starting with factory workers in Russia's major cities.

EXAM-STYLE QUESTION

A03 **A04**

SKILLS CRITICAL THINKING, REASONING, DECISION MAKING, ADAPTIVE LEARNING, CREATIVITY, INNOVATION

Study Extract B.
Extract B suggests that the Kornilov Revolt was the most important reason for the rapid increase in support for the Bolsheviks.
How far do you agree with this interpretation?
Use Extract B, Sources G and I and your own knowledge to explain your answer. **(16 marks)**

HINT

Remember to talk about differences between the extract and the sources as well as similarities. You are asked to consider the claims in the extract and see whether the evidence of the two contemporary sources and your own knowledge supports those claims.

3.3 THE BOLSHEVIK TAKEOVER

LEARNING OBJECTIVES

■ Understand the key events of the Bolshevik takeover

■ Understand the reasons for the success of the Bolsheviks, especially the roles of Lenin and Trotsky

■ Understand how the weaknesses of the Provisional Government contributed to the Bolshevik takeover.

10 October Lenin returns to Russia in secret

24–25 October The Bolsheviks take control of strategic areas of Petrograd

21 October Petrograd troops support the Military Revolutionary Committee

25–26 October The Bolsheviks take over the Winter Palace

EXTRACT C

From a history of the Russian revolution, published in 2014.

The truth is that by late October, power lay in the streets of the capital and all the Bolsheviks had to do was pick it up.

ACTIVITY

What is the author trying to say in Extract C?

KEY EVENT 1: LENIN RETURNS TO RUSSIA

Lenin and the Bolsheviks could see that the Provisional Government was close to collapse. On 10 October, Lenin secretly returned to Petrograd from Finland. In a long and stormy meeting with senior Bolsheviks, Lenin put forward the case for an armed **takeover** of power.

KEY EVENT 2: THE MILITARY REVOLUTIONARY COMMITTEE IS SET UP

Rumours spread that the Bolsheviks were planning an armed takeover, so Kerensky tried to send Bolshevik-influenced army units out of Petrograd. The Petrograd Soviet claimed that Kerensky was planning another counter-revolutionary attack, and it set up the Military Revolutionary Committee (the MRC) to bring together all the soviet-supporting soldiers in Petrograd. By 21 October, most of Petrograd's regiments promised loyalty to the MRC.

KEY EVENT 3: KERENSKY TRIES TO STOP THE BOLSHEVIKS

Kerensky ordered a **crackdown** on the Bolsheviks, closing Bolshevik newspapers, blocking river crossings between the city centre and working-class districts, calling for the arrest of the MRC. Lenin and Trotsky were quick to call this a counter-revolution. Trotsky, now as head of the Petrograd Soviet, used the MRC to take control of road and canal bridges, army headquarters and the **telegraph** office. Meanwhile, Kerensky had to travel around Petrograd by car, looking for any soldiers who would defend the Provisional Government from the Bolsheviks.

KEY EVENT 4: THE BOLSHEVIKS SEIZE CONTROL

During the night and early morning of 24–25 October, the Red Guards seized more key areas of the city. There was almost no opposition. Over the next 2 days, 25–26 October, Bolshevik soldiers climbed through the windows of the Winter Palace and arrested the remaining members of the Provisional Government. Many from the other revolutionary parties complained that the

Bolsheviks had acted without their agreement, and risked setting off a civil war that would ruin Russia and socialism. Many left the Petrograd Soviet in protest, leaving the Bolsheviks and the left-wing members of the Socialist Revolutionary Party in control of the soviet. Trotsky said that those who had left belonged in 'the dustbin of history'. On 26 October, Lenin formed a Bolshevik government called the Council of People's Commissars.

SOURCE J

This Soviet portrayal of the October Revolution shows Bolshevik soldiers attacking the Winter Palace during 25–26 October. In fact, the Bolsheviks met almost no resistance at the Winter Palace, though there was fighting for control of Moscow and Petrograd in the 10 days that followed.

ACTIVITY

Study Source J. Why do you think the artist has shown a battle to take control of the Winter Palace, whereas in fact there was very little fighting?

EXAM-STYLE QUESTION

Describe **two** features of the Bolshevik takeover in October 1917.   **(6 marks)**

A01

HINT

Make sure you give three or four lines of factual support for each feature.

REASONS FOR BOLSHEVIK SUCCESS

The main reasons why the Bolsheviks were successful in seizing power in October 1917 were:

- the role of Lenin
- failures of the Provisional Government
- the role of Trotsky.

SOURCE K

Lenin at work in his office. Lenin did not often appear in public before the October Revolution, unlike Trotsky, who made very frequent speeches.

THE ROLE OF LENIN

- Before Lenin's return to Russia from Switzerland, the Bolshevik Party agreed with other socialist parties that they should support the Provisional Government because Russia was not ready for a socialist revolution. Lenin thought differently and changed the party's view. His clear thinking and strong personality were important in shaping the outcome of events.
- Lenin's April Theses introduced radical new thinking into the Bolshevik Party; he gave its members simple but effective new slogans, such as *'Peace, Land and Bread!'*, which made a lot of sense to ordinary Russians.
- In October 1917, senior Bolsheviks could not agree on the best way for the party to seize power. Some thought the Bolsheviks should join other socialist parties and aim to get into government through the elections to the Constituent Assembly. Lenin saw things differently. He convinced other Bolsheviks that the time was right to seize power by force, and developed the strategy to make this a success.

FAILURES OF THE PROVISIONAL GOVERNMENT

By October 1917, the Provisional Government was in serious trouble. Kerensky seemed unable to take decisive action against the Bolsheviks. The main failures suffered by the Provisional Government at the time were as follows:

- The Kornilov Revolt had weakened Kerensky and weakened support for the Provisional Government. Instead, ordinary people increasingly gave their support to the Bolsheviks (and in the countryside, to the Socialist Revolutionary Party).
- The army and navy had lost all discipline and the Provisional Government could no longer count on the armed forces to maintain law and order in the cities.
- Peasants (many of them deserters from the army) were seizing land all over Russia; the Provisional Government had no way to stop this, so it lost support from landowners.

From a biography of Trotsky, published in 2003.

The October Revolution occurred in the way Trotsky had planned it, through a gradual build-up of Soviet control over key parts of the city's defences. Kerensky was defeated by the network that Trotsky helped put in place.

ACTIVITY

How important do you think the author of Extract D thought Trotsky was in bringing about the October Revolution?

In this photo, Trotsky is standing next to Lenin. Trotsky is seen smoking a cigarette. Lenin was very health-conscious and did not approve of smoking.

EXTEND YOUR KNOWLEDGE

Lenin is well known as an anti-smoker, though there are stories of him buying cigarettes in a tobacconist's when in exile in Switzerland – but refusing to pay! However, when in power he must have given up, because he is said to have theatrically opened windows whenever a colleague lit a cigarette.

■ The German army was advancing into Russia. Petrograd was in real danger of being attacked and captured by the enemy, and plans were made to move the capital to Moscow. The Bolsheviks used this opportunity to claim that Kerensky was planning to **surrender** Petrograd to the Germans.

There were also other problems. Kerensky could have acted more decisively to crush the Bolsheviks after the July Days, but he underestimated how quickly their support would grow, and did not see the danger of October 1917 until it was too late. Furthermore, he failed to introduce an elected government or to bring in radical reforms to Russia's society.

THE ROLE OF TROTSKY

■ Trotsky was the one who organised the Bolshevik takeover of power in Petrograd, following Lenin's strategy. In Moscow, the Bolsheviks' attempt to take over power was not well organised, and fighting continued for days. But in Petrograd, Trotsky's clever tactics meant the troops were used very effectively and there was very little opposition.

■ Trotsky was a hero among revolutionary socialists because of his role in the 1905 revolution. His brilliant speeches were very important in the increase in support for the Bolsheviks once he joined the party in 1917.

■ Trotsky's role as president of the Petrograd Soviet gave the Bolsheviks control of the Military Revolutionary Committee, which made it easier to get the military in Petrograd to support the takeover of power.

■ There could have been a negative reaction against the Bolsheviks because it could have been seen as though Lenin was simply seizing power for himself. Trotsky set up the takeover so it looked as if the soviets were taking control of Russia, not just the Bolsheviks.

THE CONSTITUENT ASSEMBLY AND THE TAKEOVER OF POWER

Kerensky had promised elections to the Constituent Assembly in November 1917. In the period leading up to the elections, the Bolsheviks did not think they could win because of the popularity of the Socialist Revolutionary Party among Russia's huge peasant population. Kerensky's decision therefore put pressure on Lenin to act before the November elections.

ACTIVITY

1 Create a revision poster, setting out the different reasons for Bolshevik success in October 1917. Add images to your poster to make your reasons more memorable.
2 Rank your top three reasons for Bolshevik success. Explain why you have picked those three as the most important.
3 'The most important reason for the Bolshevik's success in October 1917 was luck.' To what extent do you agree with this statement?

INTERPRETING THE BOLSHEVIK TAKEOVER OF POWER, OCTOBER 1917

One of the skills you are going to have to show in the exam is the ability to consider different interpretations of an event. The October Revolution is an event that has been interpreted in many different ways.

EXTRACT E

From a history of the Soviet Union, published in 1998.

Historians are divided between those who explain the October Revolution as a Bolshevik conspiracy or power-grab and those who emphasize the deeper social conflicts that propelled the Bolsheviks into a strong position.

The five extracts below are all interpretations of the revolution. This means each extract is saying something about the revolution from a particular point of view.

ACTIVITY

Extract E suggests that modern historians have interpreted the October Revolution in different ways. Study Extracts F to I, and answer these questions.
a Summarise the main argument made by each interpretation.
b What can you find in each interpretation to make you think that?
c Based on what you have read in this chapter, which interpretation do you think is the best? Explain why you think this.

EXTRACT F

From a history of the Russian Revolution, published in 1990.

In October, the Bolsheviks gave up on massive armed demonstrations and street skirmishes... because the crowds proved difficult to control and provoked a backlash. They relied instead on small, disciplined units of soldiers and workers under the command of... the Military Revolutionary Committee... The entire operation was carried out so smoothly and efficiently that even as it was in progress the cafes and restaurants along with the opera, theatres and cinemas were open for business and thronged with crowds in search of amusement.

EXTRACT G

From a history of the Russian Revolution, published in 1976.

In the late spring and summer of 1917, a number of factors served to increase support for the professed goals of the Bolsheviks, especially for transfer of power to the soviets. Economic conditions steadily worsened. Garrison soldiers [soldiers stationed in cities like Petrograd] became directly threatened by shipment to the front. Popular expectations of early peace and reform under the Provisional Government faded away.

EXTRACT H

From a history of the Russian Revolution, published in 1994.

A closer examination shows that the Bolsheviks had different and conflicting plans about how they would acquire political power. In general, Trotsky's vision of a gradual and cautious route dominated, with Lenin's conception of an armed uprising being implemented only belatedly and inefficiently. The Bolsheviks' conquest of power was not a single event which took place on 25 October but a process which began with the defeat of the Kornilov movement.

EXTRACT I

From a history of the Russian Revolution, published in 1996.

One of the most basic misconceptions of the Russian Revolution is that the Bolsheviks were swept to power on a tide of mass support for the party itself. The October insurrection was a coup d'état [when a small group, usually supported by the security forces, overthrows the government], actively supported by a small minority of the population (and indeed opposed by several of the Bolshevik leaders themselves). But it took place in the middle of a social revolution… The political vacuum brought about by this social revolution enabled the Bolsheviks to seize power in the cities…

SOURCE M

This painting from 1932 shows Lenin at the Bolshevik headquarters in October 1917. The artist has shown Lenin giving instructions to heavily armed Bolshevik soldiers, putting Lenin in the leading role of the revolution.

RECAP

RECALL QUESTIONS

1 Which two organisations shared state power after the February Revolution?
2 The Petrograd Soviet's 'Order Number 1' declared that the soviet had authority over which area of government?
3 Which member of the Provisional Government was first minister of war and then, after the July Days, leader of the Provisional Government?
4 Who travelled across Germany in a sealed train?
5 Complete this Bolshevik slogan: 'Peace, Land and ...'
6 Was it true or false that Germany sent the Bolsheviks money to fund their activities?
7 What was Lenin forced to do at the end of the July Days?
8 Whom did Kerensky appoint as commander-in-chief of the Russian army on 18 July 1917, only to dismiss him again shortly afterwards?
9 The Petrograd Soviet set up the MRC after the Kornilov Revolt to guard against future counter-revolutionary attacks. What does MRC stand for?
10 Which building, a former palace, did the Bolsheviks take over in the early morning of 26 October, arresting the remaining members of the Provisional Government?

CHECKPOINT

STRENGTHEN
S1 Identify two reasons for the Bolsheviks' success in October 1917.
S2 Why did General Kornilov's revolt strengthen the support for the Bolsheviks?
S3 Explain what the Bolshevik slogan 'Peace, Land and Bread' was promising.

CHALLENGE
C1 Historians have interpreted the Bolshevik takeover of power in many different ways. Describe two contrasting interpretations you have studied.
C2 Why do you think some Bolsheviks disagreed with Lenin's plan to take power in Russia by force?
C3 Some historians have argued that the Bolsheviks were able to overthrow the Provisional Government because of Trotsky's brilliance. What do you think they mean by this?

SUMMARY

- The Provisional Government and Petrograd Soviet set up a system called Dual Control.
- Order Number 1 gave the Petrograd Soviet control over military matters.
- The war continued and the June Offensive was a disaster.
- There was an unsuccessful uprising (the July Days) and Lenin fled to Finland.
- The Bolsheviks worked to win popularity with their slogan 'Peace, Land and Bread'.
- Kerensky invited Kornilov to help him stop unrest in Petrograd.
- The Bolsheviks' role in stopping Kornilov gained them support.
- The Bolsheviks staged a revolution.
- On 26 October 1917, Lenin formed a Bolshevik government.

EXAM GUIDANCE: PART (A) QUESTIONS

A01

Question to be answered: Describe **two** features of either the First Duma (1906) or the July Days (1917). (6 marks)

1 | **Analysis Question 1: What is the question type testing?**
In this question, you have to demonstrate that you have knowledge and understanding of the key features and characteristics of the period studied. In this section we are going to look at the the July Days, so it is knowledge and understanding of the events in July 1917.

2 | **Analysis Question 2: What do I have to do to answer the question well?**
Obviously you have to choose one of the two options and write about it! But this isn't just a case of writing everything you know. You have to write about two features, which are 'aspects' or 'characteristics'. We might even say that, if you were allowed to put sub-headings in your answers, both features would be the sub-headings you would put.

3 | **Analysis Question 3: Are there any techniques I can use to make it very clear that I am doing what is needed to be successful?**
This is a 6-mark question and you need to make sure you leave enough time to answer the other two questions fully (they are worth 24 marks in total). Therefore, you need to get straight into writing your answer. The question asks for two features, so it's a good idea to write one paragraph for each, and to begin each paragraph with phrases like 'One feature was…' and 'Another feature was…'. You will get 1 mark for each feature you identify, and up to 2 marks for giving detail to support each feature. This gives the maximum of 6 marks.

You have to demonstrate knowledge, so make sure you back up your paragraphs with as much detailed knowledge as you have. But remember that you are not writing an essay here. You are giving enough detail to pick up 2 extra marks on each feature you have identified.

Answer A

The July Days were an uprising against the government, which took place between 3 and 7 July 1917. Tens of thousands of workers and soldiers marched with banners calling for power to be handed to the soviets.

What are the strengths and weaknesses of Answer B?

It is a basic answer and lacks detail. Although this question does not require extensive writing or explanation, to be well-rewarded, there needs to be more factual detail than is provided. Also, only one feature is described.

Answer B

One feature of the July Days was that it was an uprising which took place between 3 and 7 July 1917. It was a protest by anarchist revolutionaries, who persuaded disillusioned soldiers and discontented workers to join in their anti-government demonstration. Tens of thousands of workers and soldiers marched with banners calling for power to be handed to the soviets. Although the Bolsheviks had originally been against the demonstration, they quickly decided that the time had come to overthrow the Provisional Government in the same way that the Tsar had been overthrown in February.

Another feature was that the uprising did not succeed. It did not have the support of the Petrograd Soviet and other political parties were suspicious of the Bolsheviks. But the Bolsheviks met with the leaders of the Petrograd Soviet and agreed on a way they could work together to overthrow the Provisional Government. However, the uprising was not successful. Poor weather meant the demonstrating crowds began to disperse and the government brought troops back from the front to deal with the uprising. Hundreds of Bolsheviks were arrested, including Trotsky, and Lenin was forced to flee to Finland.

What are the strengths and weaknesses of Answer B?

This is an excellent answer. Two features are identified (note how the terms 'one feature' and 'another feature' are used, and each one is well supported with factual information. For a 6-mark question that needs to be answered in limited time, the answer contains more detailed support than might be expected.

Challenge a friend

Use the Student Book to set a part (a) question for a friend. Then look at the answer. Does it do the following things?

- ☐ Identify two features
- ☐ Make it clear that two features are being covered
- ☐ Give 3–4 lines of detailed information to support the feature.

If it does, you can tell your friend that the answer is very good!

4. THE BOLSHEVIK CONSOLIDATION OF POWER AND THE CIVIL WAR

LEARNING OBJECTIVES

■ Understand the main ways in which the Bolsheviks tried to strengthen their control of Russia and the nationalities of the old Russian empire

■ Understand the reasons for the Treaty of Brest-Litovsk, and its consequences

■ Understand the key events of the Civil War and the reasons for the Bolshevik victory.

The Bolsheviks were able to take over control of Russia in October 1917 from the Provisional Government without difficulty. Holding on to power, however, was a much more difficult challenge. The Bolsheviks now had to deliver on some enormous promises, including an end to Russia's involvement in the First World War. Socialist theory predicted that the Russian revolution would be rapidly followed by workers' revolutions in other countries, especially heavily industrialised Germany. But this failed to happen. The Bolsheviks negotiated a treaty with Germany to end the war between them, but at an enormous cost to Russia. Fury with the Bolsheviks for signing the Treaty of Brest-Litovsk was a major cause of the Russian Civil War, in which the Bolsheviks were attacked by different groups that all opposed their rule over Russia.

4.1 THE BOLSHEVIK CONSOLIDATION OF POWER

LEARNING OBJECTIVES

- Understand some of the problems facing the Bolsheviks after October 1917
- Understand the Bolsheviks' early decrees and what they aimed to achieve
- Understand the Bolsheviks' treatment of the Constituent Assembly and its consequences.

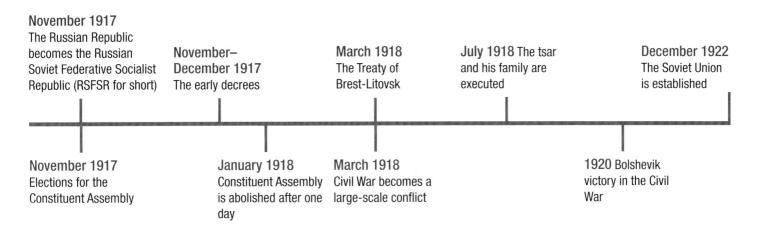

November 1917
The Russian Republic becomes the Russian Soviet Federative Socialist Republic (RSFSR for short)

November–December 1917
The early decrees

March 1918
The Treaty of Brest-Litovsk

July 1918 The tsar and his family are executed

December 1922
The Soviet Union is established

November 1917
Elections for the Constituent Assembly

January 1918
Constituent Assembly is abolished after one day

March 1918
Civil War becomes a large-scale conflict

1920 Bolshevik victory in the Civil War

Although the Bolsheviks had been successful in taking control away from the Provisional Government, Lenin's party faced many problems in strengthening its control over Russia. The area of the Russian Soviet Federative Socialist Republic (RSFSR), which the Bolsheviks had control over in 1917, was actually very small: it only included Petrograd, Moscow and the region in between the two cities. Winning Moscow alone had taken the Bolsheviks weeks of fighting. At the same time, many other areas started to organise their own local governments that were strongly opposed to the Bolsheviks.

THE PROBLEM OF THE CONSTITUENT ASSEMBLY

Lenin had promised that, once the Bolsheviks were in power, they would immediately hold elections for the Constituent Assembly. This would bring about the democratic election of a new government for Russia that the Provisional Government had failed to deliver. But there was a problem with holding free elections: in the countryside, the Social Revolutionaries were still much more popular than the Bolsheviks and might win more seats than them.

But, if the Bolsheviks did not immediately hold elections, people would probably stop supporting them. Some Bolsheviks thought the best way forward would be for all the revolutionary parties to work together in the new Constituent Assembly. Lenin did not agree.

The Council of the People's Commissars (known also as Sovnarkom) in 1917. Sovnarkom was the government of Russia, established after the Bolsheviks seized power in the October Revolution. Its first chairman was Lenin and all its members were Bolsheviks.

THE PROBLEM OF THE BOLSHEVIKS' PROMISES

It was not just the issue of the Constituent Assembly that caused problems for the Bolsheviks. A major part of the Bolsheviks' appeal had been their promise of 'Peace, Land and Bread', and 'All Power to the Soviets'. However, carrying out these promises in reality was very difficult for the Bolsheviks to achieve, especially if they wanted to **consolidate** their power. Below are some examples of their struggles.

■ Promise of 'peace': It was not possible for Lenin simply to end Russia's involvement in the war and achieve peace; none of Russia's former allies would agree to **negotiate** with the Bolsheviks, which meant Russia would have to negotiate a separate peace deal with Germany. Since Germany knew that the Bolsheviks were desperate to leave the war, a peace deal would be very costly for Russia.

■ Promise of 'land': The Bolsheviks had promised land, which the peasants understood as meaning they would take all the land for themselves. However, giving up land to the peasants risked weakening Bolshevik control, not strengthening it. The Bolsheviks were a party of the industrial workers and believed in state-run farms; it was the Social Revolutionaries who would benefit from a stronger peasantry in Russia.

■ Promise of 'bread': Like Lenin, the Bolsheviks believed the state should be able to take food from the peasants to make sure the workers had everything they needed. This would be the easiest way to end food shortages in the cities, but would also be difficult if the peasants had control of all the land.

■ Promise of 'all power to the Soviets': When the Bolshevik Party took control, it was only supposed to run post-revolutionary Russia for a short time, until the workers and peasants were ready to run the country for themselves through local, regional and national soviets. But to deliver on this promise would mean the Bolsheviks giving up control of Russia.

Despite their earlier promises, and whatever the Bolshevik Party may have intended, it went on to rule for seven decades in ways that were very different from what had been promised in 1917. Instead of democracy, there was one-party rule. Instead of giving all power to the soviets, the party kept a tight hold on power and ruled in a system that went on to be just as **authoritarian** as the tsarist autocracy.

As part of consolidating their power, in 1917 the Bolsheviks established four 'soviet socialist republics', one for Russia, one for Ukraine, one for Belorussia and one for Transcaucasia (Georgia, Armenia and Azerbaijan). In December 1922, these republics were grouped together as the Union of Soviet Socialist Republics or USSR (often called the Soviet Union). Other parts of the old Russian Empire were joined to the Soviet Union in later years.

THE 1917 DECREES

Because the Petrograd Soviet still had many Mensheviks and Socialist Revolutionaries as members, Lenin used a newly created body to govern Russia instead, after the October Revolution. This body was known as *Sovnarkom* – the shortened version of the Russian name for the Council of People's Commissars (CPC for short in English). The CPC was completely controlled by the Bolsheviks.

Immediately after taking control in October 1917, the CPC passed important **decrees** that set out how Russia was to be governed under Bolshevik control. Historians call these the 'early decrees', because they happened very early on in the Bolshevik rule of Russia.

Decree on Peace
- Said all countries involved in the war should seek peace
- Armistice for Russian troops

Decree on Land
- Land taken from wealthy landowners now belonged to the peasants
- In December, Church land was nationalised, too

The early decrees (November–December 1917)

Decree on workers' rights
- **Decree on Work** – 8-hour day
- **Decree on Unemployment** – unemployment insurance for those unable to work
- **Decree on Workers' Control** – workers' committees now ran their own factories

Decree on Nationalities
- All the different peoples of the old Russian empire could have their own governments
- However, these governments remained under Bolshevik control

▶ **Figure 4.1** The early decrees

DECREE ON LAND

The Decree on Land abolished the private ownership of land. Now all the land in Russia belonged to the state, and would be given to those who farmed it – the peasants. At first, this decree applied to land owned by private landlords and to land owned by the tsar; by December 1917 it was extended to all the land owned by the Church.

The Decree on Land meant the peasants were now more likely to support the Bolshevik government. However, the peasants had already taken so much land from the landlords that in many places this decree did not change anything for the peasants apart from making their takeovers legal.

SOURCE B

A Bolshevik propaganda painting showing a soldier reading out Lenin's decree that private property was abolished and land would go to the peasants. The majority of peasants at this time were not able to read for themselves.

ACTIVITY

Study Source B and its caption. How does the artist show that rural life in Russia was still very undeveloped in 1917?

KEY TERMS

armistice a truce; an end to fighting for an agreed period of time

treaty a formal written agreement between two or more countries or governments

DECREE ON PEACE

This was a call for all nations involved in the war to start peace negotiations. Lenin's decree called for an immediate **armistice** and ordered the government to agree peace with Germany but without giving up any of Russia's territory or making compensation to Germany.

Lenin was confident that workers in other European countries would soon lead revolutions against their own governments. Once these revolutions started, Lenin thought, the governments of countries like Germany would be keen to agree peace terms with Russia. But Russian conservatives, especially officers in the army and navy, did not believe for a moment that Germany would agree to sign any peace **treaty** with Russia without getting Russian territory in exchange. The Bolsheviks' unrealistic approach to achieving peace was significant, because it was an important factor in bringing about the Civil War in 1918.

DECREE ON NATIONALITIES

This decree was meant to assure all the different ethnic minorities within the old Russian empire that the Bolsheviks would not impose Russian control on them; the idea was that the groups would have their own choice of government. This decree was significant, because it showed how worried the Bolsheviks were at the thought of ethnic minorities, such as the Ukrainians, using the opportunity of a weak Russian government to break away and become independent countries. It wasn't until 1922 that the different 'soviet socialist republics' were brought together under Bolshevik Party rule as the USSR (see page 67).

DECREES ON WORKERS' RIGHTS

A number of decrees were aimed at immediately improving conditions for industrial workers – the Bolsheviks' most important supporters.

- The Decree on Work (12 November) brought in an 8-hour working day: a key demand of striking workers since the 1905 revolution and before. It also set a maximum of 48 hours of work a week for industrial workers. New rules for overtime and holidays were also set out by the decree.
- The Decree on Unemployment (14 November) was about providing insurance for all workers so that they would still get money to live on if they were injured at work, if they were sick or became unemployed.
- The Decree on Workers' Control (27 December) put all the factories under the control of workers' soviets. As with the Decree on Land, this was about legalising something that was already happening.

OTHER MEASURES

The Council of the People's Commissars passed other measures, which not only increased their control of the country, but also reflected Bolshevik thinking about society in general. Marriage and divorce, for example, became civil matters – they were no longer related to the Church; women were declared equal to men and could now own property; ranks and saluting in the army were abolished, as were titles and class distinctions. Most significantly, opposition press was banned and a new secret police force, the Cheka, was set up.

EXAM-STYLE QUESTION

A01

Describe **two** features of the Bolsheviks' 1917 decrees. **(6 marks)**

> **HINT**
>
> Remember that 'two features' doesn't just mean giving two decrees. Try to put your answer into two categories – such as land or unemployment – and then provide detail to support each one.

THE CONSTITUENT ASSEMBLY ELECTIONS

On 27 October, 2 days after the start of the October Revolution, Lenin announced that elections to the Constituent Assembly would take place on 12 November. But when the election results came in, they were a disaster for the Bolsheviks. The Socialist Revolutionaries were the winners with 53 per cent of the votes. The Bolsheviks had just under one quarter of the votes.

THE RESULTS OF THE ELECTIONS

The Bolsheviks had done well in the major industrial cities, getting nearly half of all the votes in Petrograd and Moscow. They also did very well among ordinary soldiers. But in the countryside, the Bolsheviks generally did very badly, just as they had feared. Despite the Bolsheviks' Decree on Land, most peasants voted for the Socialist Revolutionaries, the party that had been campaigning for the peasants and for land reform for decades.

THE BOLSHEVIKS' RESPONSE TO THE ELECTIONS

The other socialist parties had hoped that the Bolsheviks would accept the result and join them in a socialist parliament, deciding on Russia's future together. But the Bolsheviks rejected this, and rejected the results of the elections. Lenin now criticised the Constituent Assembly as a threat to the

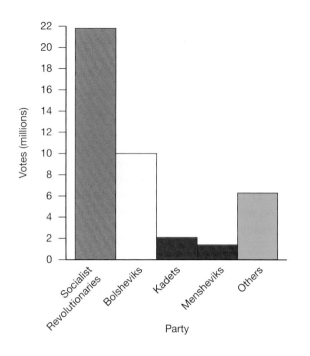

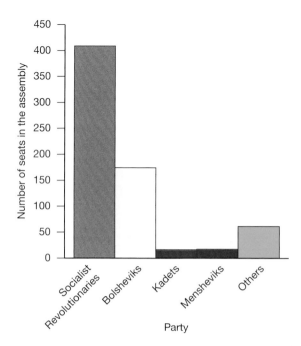

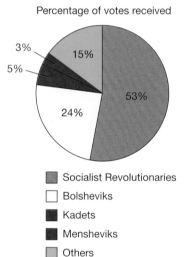

Percentage of votes received

- Socialist Revolutionaries
- Bolsheviks
- Kadets
- Mensheviks
- Others

revolution and a threat to the soviets: how could all power go to *both* the soviets *and* the Constituent Assembly? Everyone waited to see what the Bolsheviks would do.

CLOSING THE CONSTITUENT ASSEMBLY

The first meeting of the Constituent Assembly took place on 5 January 1918. The Council of People's Commissars made a proposal for the assembly to pass. This proposal summarised all the Bolsheviks' key decrees: the Decree on Land, the Decree on Peace, the Decree on Workers' Control and the principle of all power to the soviets. The Constituent Assembly rejected the proposal by a majority of over 100 votes. It realised that granting all power to the soviets would make the Constituent Assembly irrelevant.

Lenin took the rejection as an opportunity to claim this proved that the Constituent Assembly did not represent the will of the people. In fact, according to Lenin, it was dominated by counter-revolutionaries: those who wanted to bring back capitalism. If the Constituent Assembly opposed the will of the soviets, then the Constituent Assembly had to go. The Bolshevik delegates walked out of the assembly in protest, and Lenin announced that the Constituent Assembly would be dissolved. The next day, Lenin brought in the Red Guards to prevent the assembly from opening. Shortly afterwards, all opposition political parties were banned in Russia, including the Socialist Revolutionaries, the Mensheviks and the Kadets. Leaders of opposition parties were arrested as enemies of the people. The Bolshevik Party was the only one safe from this ban.

From a conversation with Lenin in October 1917, recorded by Trotsky in his memoirs.

'On the very first day, if not the first hour of the Revolution,' relates Trotsky, 'Lenin brought up the question of the Constituent Assembly. "We must postpone the elections. We must extend the right of suffrage [the right to vote] to those who have reached… eighteen years. We must outlaw from voting the adherents of Kornilov and the Kadets," said Lenin.

'We tried to argue with him that it would not look right. We ourselves had accused the Provisional Government of delaying the elections to the Constituent Assembly.'

'"Nonsense," Lenin replied. "It is facts that are important, not words."'

From Lenin's announcement of the end of the Constituent Assembly, written on 6 January 1918.

The working classes learned by experience that the old bourgeois parliamentary system… was absolutely incompatible with the aim of achieving socialism… [O]nly class institutions (such as the Soviets) were capable of overcoming the resistance of the propertied classes and of laying the foundations of socialist society. To relinquish [let go of] the… power of the Soviets, to relinquish the Soviet Republic won by the people, for the sake of the bourgeois… Constituent Assembly, would now be a step backwards and would cause the collapse of the October workers' and peasants' revolution.

ACTIVITY

What reasons were there for Lenin and the Bolsheviks to want to achieve an end to Russia's involvement in the war? Think about the events of 1917 to help you answer this.

EXAM-STYLE QUESTION

A03

SKILLS ANALYSIS, ADAPTIVE LEARNING, CREATIVITY

Study Sources C and D.
How far does Source C support the evidence of Source D about Lenin's attitude towards the Constituent Assembly?
Explain your answer.   (8 marks)

HINT

Remember that you have to provide evidence for your answer. If you say that Source C supports Source D, then also say which part of Source C supports which part of Source D!

THE TREATY OF BREST-LITOVSK

BACKGROUND TO THE TREATY

Following the Decree on Peace, there was a ceasefire between Russia and Germany while a conference was organised to discuss an end to the war. This conference was held at the German army's headquarters in Brest-Litovsk (which was then an area in Poland; now the area is known as Brest and is a part of Belarus). Russia's old allies – Britain, France and the USA – did not attend. This meant Russia had to negotiate a separate peace treaty with Germany and Germany's allies on its own. Negotiations began on 22 December 1917.

Lenin gave Trotsky the responsibility of negotiating the treaty with Germany. Trotsky was certain that a revolution in Germany was about to occur and he kept discussions going for 2 months. Unfortunately, no German revolution happened. Trotsky then announced that, although Russia would not continue fighting, it was not going to give up any land or pay any compensation to Germany for war losses. Trotsky thought the German army was exhausted, and so would not be able to continue fighting. However, this was not correct. The German response to Trotsky's announcement was to end the armistice and continue their invasion of Russia. The Russian army could do little to stop the Germans, who now looked likely to capture Petrograd. Moscow was made the capital city in case this happened.

THE SIGNING OF THE TREATY

Lenin demanded that Trotsky achieve peace with Germany at any price. He recognised that Russia did not have the military strength to fight the Germans. If the Germans beat the Russians, the Bolsheviks would be finished and so would their revolution. Lenin was also more concerned with defeating opposition to the Bolsheviks within Russia than fighting other countries. He knew that the Bolsheviks could not afford to fight a civil war in Russia *and* the Germans at the same time.

Because the Germans knew the Russians were desperate to leave the war, they set extremely harsh terms for peace between the two countries. Russia had to give up a huge area of its former western territories, which included Ukraine and the Baltic provinces, Finland and parts of Poland. Russia also lost Georgia – the homeland of the future leader, Stalin.

Giving up the territories meant Russia had to lose:
- 74 per cent of its coal mines and iron ore
- 50 per cent of its industry
- 26 per cent of its railway network
- 27 per cent of its farmland
- 26 per cent of its population (which was 62 million at the time).

On top of all this, Russia also had to pay the Germans 300 million gold roubles.

Despite the harsh terms, the Treaty of Brest-Litovsk was signed on 3 March 1918.

CONSEQUENCES OF THE TREATY

Throughout Russia, the Treaty of Brest-Litovsk was seen as a shameful way to achieve peace. Half of Tsar Nicholas's empire had been lost, along with much of its most important resources. Russia was a far weaker country than it had been before the Bolshevik revolution. The loss of some of Russia's most productive farmland meant that the treaty had effectively made Russia's food shortage situation even worse. People began to leave the starving cities and return to the countryside, so they could grow their own food. By June 1918, 1 million people had left Petrograd and the number of people working there had shrunk by 60 per cent. There was a lot of opposition to the treaty up and down the country.

Although front-line soldiers were pleased that the war had ended, and the Russian people in general were relieved that the threat of German invasion was over, most Russians were devastated by what they had lost. Many

EXTEND YOUR KNOWLEDGE

TALKING COSTS!

The German negotiators at Brest-Litovsk pretended to be very friendly towards the Russian negotiating team. They drank with the Russians, and praised them for getting rid of the Provisional Government and for ending the war. The inexperienced Russians fell for the trick and told the 'friendly' Germans far too much about the situation with their military, the problems within Russia, and about their own government. The German team were then able to report all this secret information back to their own government and army commanders.

Key

☐ Area occupied by Germany, Austria-Hungary, the Ottoman Empire and Bulgaria after the Treaty of Brest-Litovsk.

▲ N

0   200
km

▶ **Figure 4.2** The area of Russia given to Germany and its allies after the Treaty of Brest-Litovsk

SOURCE E

Lenin commenting on the terms of the Treaty of Brest-Litovsk.

Their knees are on our chest, and our position is hopeless. This peace must be accepted as a respite enabling us to prepare a decisive resistance to the bourgeoisie and imperialists.

ACTIVITY

What do you think Lenin meant by his comments in Source E?

conservatives in Russia were now convinced that they had to fight to stop the Bolsheviks so that Russia could be saved from further humiliation and destruction. This meant that the Treaty of Brest-Litovsk was a major cause of the Civil War. Even the Bolshevik Party itself was split by the treaty; those who had wanted to bring about a socialist revolution complained bitterly that all the treaty did was help Germany survive as an imperialist power. Lenin, however, firmly believed the Bolsheviks had no choice.

SOURCE F

Russian troops withdrawing from the front line following the end of Russia's involvement in the First World War, after the Treaty of Brest-Litovsk in March 1918.

4.2 THE CIVIL WAR

LEARNING OBJECTIVES

- Understand the reasons for the Russian Civil War
- Understand the key features of the Civil War
- Understand the reasons why the Bolsheviks won the Civil War.

REASONS FOR THE CIVIL WAR

There were many groups within Russia who opposed the Bolsheviks:
- **monarchists** who wanted to put the tsar back into power
- upper-class and middle-class people who were in danger of losing everything under the Bolsheviks
- supporters of the Constituent Assembly who hated the way the Bolsheviks had turned Russia into a **dictatorship**
- other nationalities within the old Russian empire who wanted independence from Russian control.

The Treaty of Brest-Litovsk was a major cause of the Civil War. Even many of the Bolsheviks' opponents saw it as such a shocking national disgrace that they had to join together with others to fight the Bolsheviks.

KEY TERM

dictatorship rule by one person, a dictator, who has complete power

SIDES IN THE CIVIL WAR

There were many different groups fighting in the Civil War, but the two main sides were known as the Reds and the Whites. The Reds were the Bolsheviks. The Whites were a collection of different groups who wanted to get rid of the Bolsheviks.

EXTRACT A

From a history of the Soviet Union, published in 1998.

The civil war was not only a war of armies but of ordinary people who had to choose which army to fight for and whether to hold their positions under fire or desert [run away].

ACTIVITY

People do not normally have 'to choose which army to fight for' in a war. Why did they have to do so in this war?

THE REDS

The Bolsheviks were a very organised and disciplined group. They brought their organisational skills and ruthless attitude to the way they fought the Civil War. As commissar for war, Trotsky was now in charge of fighting the Civil War. He devoted himself entirely to winning the war, whatever the cost.

Trotsky organised the creation of a Bolshevik army called the Red Army. At first, it was based on adding more volunteers to the Red Guard (see page 50), but Trotsky quickly realised that the Red Guard was not the right model to win the war. The Red Guard was made up of several thousand volunteer workers who were given a rifle and a little military training. For the Civil War, Trotsky needed a traditional army with trained soldiers obeying orders from experienced officers. To do this, Trotsky recruited officers from the tsar's old army. Every one of these officers was supervised by a Bolshevik political commissar; the officers were also told that their families would suffer if they betrayed the Red Army in any way. Discipline was extremely harsh throughout the Red Army. The political commissars often executed any soldier who did not attack when ordered to. Deserters were also executed.

Compulsory military service was introduced in May 1918 in areas controlled by the Bolsheviks. By 1921, there were 5.4 million men in the Red Army. One factor that encouraged men to sign up was that food supplies went to the Red Army first.

SOURCE G

This image shows men being conscripted into the Red Army in 1918.

THE WHITES

The Whites were made up of all the different groups fighting to defeat the Reds. These different groups often had very little in common with each other, except for their opposition to the Bolsheviks. For example, the Whites included the Socialist Revolutionaries who wanted to bring back the Constituent Assembly, ultra-conservatives who wanted the tsar to return to the throne, and army officers who were angered by the Treaty of Brest-Litovsk. Sometimes these different groups fought each other as well as the Bolsheviks.

There were four main White armies, each attacking the Reds from a different region of Russia.
- In Siberia, the army was led by Admiral Kolchak.
- Attacking the Reds from Estonia in the north west was an army led by General Yudenich.
- In the south, General Denikin led a force of ex-army officers and liberals (Kadets, for example); General Wrangel took over this army in 1920.
- In Samara, south-central Russia, the People's Army of Komuch included supporters of the Constituent Assembly.

THE GREENS

Although the Reds and the Whites were the main two sides in the Civil War, there were also other groups involved. Most of these were peasant armies

EXTEND YOUR KNOWLEDGE

WHY 'THE WHITES'?

The Bolsheviks called their opponents 'the Whites' because officers in the tsarist army wore white uniforms, and those fighting in the White armies were often led by ex-tsarist army generals.

who joined together to fight for control for their own local areas. Known as the Greens, these people would defend their own areas, but it was very rare for them to advance to fight anywhere else. The best-known Green leader was Nestor Makhno. He was a Ukrainian anarchist who was fighting, like many other Greens, for independence from Russia. At different times, Makhno's army fought both the Red and the Whites.

INVOLVEMENT OF OTHER COUNTRIES

Other countries also became involved in the Civil War. For example, Britain sent supplies worth a hundred million pounds to the Whites. Britain wanted Russia back in the war and British politicians were also very worried about the spread of Bolshevism through Europe. Japan, on the other hand, sent 70,000 troops to eastern Siberia to try to take some land from Russia during this period of unrest, and the USA ended up sending troops to the same region to stop Japan from doing this. An armed force of 50,000 men from the Czech Republic and Slovenia, called the Czech Legion, took control of large stretches of the Trans-Siberian Railway.

ACTIVITY

Use the information in the section entitled 'Sides in the Civil War' to start a list of features of the Russian Civil War, using the following categories or other categories you come up with for yourself:
- different sides in the Civil War
- leaders of the Civil War
- areas involved in the Civil War
- aims of the different forces involved in the Civil War
- key features of the Red Army
- the role of Trotsky in the Civil War.

When you've read the next section, you may continue expanding this list.

KEY EVENTS OF THE CIVIL WAR

The Russian Civil War was a very complicated conflict, with armies advancing and retreating, and cities being captured first by one side and then the other; countries that were once part of the Russian empire were declaring independence, while foreign powers like the USA, Germany and the UK were sending in troops and then withdrawing them. Russia's defeat by Germany in the First World War also had an effect on the Civil War.

KEY EVENT 1: TREATY OF BREST-LITOVSK, 3 MARCH 1918

The signing of the Treaty of Brest-Litovsk united opposition to the Bolsheviks both in Russia and in other countries. Without Russia in the war, Germany would be able to concentrate all its troops on the Western Front, and that risked defeat for the British empire, France and (from April 1918) the USA. Because of this, those countries gave the Whites a lot of support – support that boosted their successes against the Reds.

KEY EVENT 2: TROTSKY BECOMES WAR COMMISSAR, 13 MARCH 1918

This was a key event in the Civil War because Trotsky was very important in organising the Red Army, ensuring discipline and keeping army morale high.

KEY EVENT 3: INVOLVEMENT OF THE CZECH LEGION, MAY 1918

The Czech Legion (see previous page) was on its way out of Russia when Trotsky ordered them to give up their weapons. The Czech Legion refused, took control of large sections of the Trans-Siberian railroad and joined forces with Socialist Revolutionaries. This was a key event because the Czech Legion was a large and experienced military force and it increased the threat to the Reds.

SOURCE H

Czech Legion soldiers on an armoured train in 1918.

EXTEND YOUR KNOWLEDGE

THE EXECUTION OF THE ROMANOVS

After a week of abuse and ill-treatment, members of the royal family were put to death by the Red Army. Tsar Nicholas, his wife Alexandra and their five children (Olga, Tatiana, Maria, Anastasia and Alexei), together with their servants, were brutally murdered. Their bodies were soaked in sulphuric acid, thrown down a mine shaft and set on fire. When they were found there was little left of the bodies, though among the remains was a finger and some false teeth. Several of the princesses are said to have survived slightly longer than the rest of the family because they had sewn jewels into the clothing for safekeeping, which gave some protection from the bullets.

KEY EVENT 4: EXECUTION OF THE ROYAL FAMILY, 17 JULY 1918

Nicholas II and his family were being held prisoner in the city of Yekaterinburg in 1918. When the White forces, joined by the Czech Legion, arrived close to the city, the Bolsheviks shot Nicholas, his wife and children, as well as four servants. Many members of the Whites had wanted the monarchy to be restored, while Nicholas could have brought a lot more support to the Whites, so the Bolsheviks killed the royal family in case they were captured by the Whites.

KEY EVENT 5: FANYA KAPLAN SHOOTS LENIN, 30 AUGUST 1918

Fanya Kaplan was a radical Socialist Revolutionary who wanted to assassinate Lenin as a traitor to the revolution for shutting down the Constituent Assembly. She shot him three times, seriously wounding him, but he survived.

This was a key event in the Civil War because it led to the Red Terror. The Red Terror was a campaign in which the Bolsheviks used their secret police, the Cheka, to arrest suspected opponents and execute them without trial. Once the Red Army had taken control of an area from the Whites, the Cheka would often go around frightening the people living there to make sure they supported the Reds.

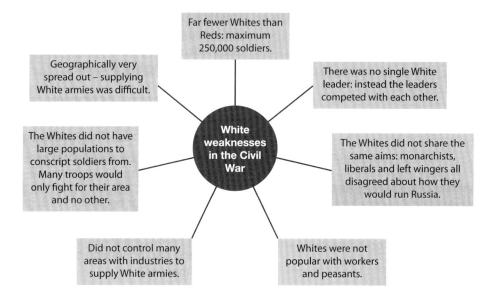

▶ Figure 4.4 White weaknesses in the Civil War

RED STRENGTHS IN THE CIVIL WAR

Despite the Bolsheviks' insecure position in 1918, the Reds had several key advantages that helped them win the Civil War in 1920.

One key strength was the size of the Red Army. Conscription meant it grew rapidly: it had over 3 million men by 1920 and over 5 million by 1921. This large size was vital for success because the Reds were being attacked from many different directions: in 1920, the Red Army was fighting on 16 different fronts.

Another strength was Leon Trotsky. Not only was it his vision that had created the Red Army, Trotsky also introduced the strict discipline that kept the Red Army together, and boosted army morale by constantly travelling from front to front in a famous armoured train. His leadership brought the Reds together and made sure they were organised.

While the Whites suffered from being out on the borders of Russia, the Reds had the advantage of a central location. This was yet another strength, as it meant easy access to Russia's industries (for essential military supplies) and easy access to the railway network, which made transportation of supplies and people easier even though the Red Army had to defend lots of different fronts. Having a central location as the base meant that the Red troops and their supplies had to travel only relatively short distances from one front to another, compared to the long distances that the Whites had to travel. Holding the centre of Russia meant access to the country's main population centres, which made it easier to recruit soldiers.

Propaganda was another important reason for the Reds' success. While some of the White leaders had no time for propaganda, the Reds used extremely striking images and powerful slogans to convince people to support them. For example, according to Red propaganda, the Whites would take away peasant land. The Reds also claimed that the foreigners helping the Whites were Russia's enemies, who wanted to invade Russia.

SOURCE I

This poster criticises the involvement of Western countries in Russia's Civil War. It shows Western powers holding the leashes of their 'dogs', which are labelled with the names of three White generals: Denikin, Kolchak and Yudenich.

EXTRACT B

From a history of the Soviet Union, published in 1998.

At least 1 million people died in combat or from White or Red acts of terror during the Russian civil war. Several million more died from disease, hunger and the cold. About a million people left the country and never returned. The Red victory had been earned with enormous sacrifice and pain on all sides.

ACTIVITY

What impression does Extract B give of the Civil War?

Finally, while Trotsky led the Red Army, Lenin focused on tackling the enormous economic problems facing Russia, especially food shortages and falling industrial production. Lenin brought in a policy known as War Communism, which put the state directly in charge of production in Russia. This made sure the army received enough food. You will find out more about War Communism in the next chapter.

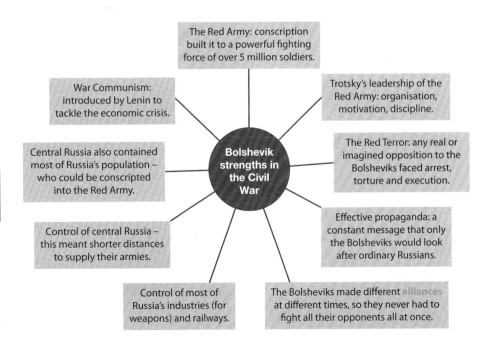

The Red Army: conscription built it to a powerful fighting force of over 5 million soldiers.

Trotsky's leadership of the Red Army: organisation, motivation, discipline.

The Red Terror: any real or imagined opposition to the Bolsheviks faced arrest, torture and execution.

Effective propaganda: a constant message that only the Bolsheviks would look after ordinary Russians.

The Bolsheviks made different alliances at different times, so they never had to fight all their opponents all at once.

Control of most of Russia's industries (for weapons) and railways.

Control of central Russia – this meant shorter distances to supply their armies.

Central Russia also contained most of Russia's population – who could be conscripted into the Red Army.

War Communism: introduced by Lenin to tackle the economic crisis.

Bolshevik strengths in the Civil War

▶ **Figure 4.5** Bolshevik strengths in the Civil War

IMPACT OF THE RED TERROR

Following the assassination attempt on Lenin (see page 77), the Bolsheviks used the secret police, the Cheka, in a campaign known as the Red Terror on their opponents, wherever they might be hiding. It is estimated that nearly 300,000 people, including the tsar and his family, were killed by the Cheka between 1918 and 1920. Whenever the Red Army captured an area from the Whites, the Cheka would be sent in to punish (usually by execution) anyone they thought had helped the Whites. The aim was to make people too frightened of the Cheka to oppose the Bolsheviks.

ACTIVITY

1 Figures 4.4 and 4.5 show nine Red strengths and seven White weaknesses. From each diagram, choose three points you think are most important. Then, out of the six points you have chosen, pick three that are the most important of all. Make sure you can justify your choices.

2 Explain why commissars were important in the Bolshevik victory in the Civil War.

3 A senior Bolshevik once said of the Civil War: 'We were always for revolutionary war. The bayonet is an essential necessity for introducing communism.' To what extent do you think the Bolsheviks welcomed the Civil War as a way of reinforcing their control of Russia?

SOURCE J

A Bolshevik poster from 1919 with the slogan, 'Long live the three-million-man Red Army'. The poster shows the Red Army equipped with the very latest military technology when in fact the Red Army was generally armed with poor-quality weapons.

SOURCE K

From an order sent out by Trotsky on 15 August 1918.

Citizens of towns temporarily captured by the Czechs and White Guards are still subject to the laws of the Soviet Republic…

Anyone who, during the rule of the Czechs and White Guards, has collaborated with them will be shot.

The property… of participants in the bourgeois revolt, and of their accomplices, will be confiscated.

Out of this property, compensation will be paid to the families of workers and peasants who fell under the blows of the counter-revolutionaries, and also to all working people generally who suffered by the bourgeois revolt.

SOURCE L

From an order sent out by Trotsky on 28 August 1918 after the city of Kazan was captured by the Whites and Czech Legion.

Workers and peasants! The Soviet troops will not let the Russian White Guards sell you to foreign capital. We will not let the landlords take the land from the peasants. We will not let the degenerates [corrupt people] of the Romanov dynasty take power into their hands. We will not let the Czechoslovak mercenaries rule the roost on Russian soil. Kazan will soon be torn from the hands of the counter-revolution and the Czechoslovak bands.

Be prepared, workers and honest citizens of Kazan! The moment is near when our foes will be crushed and working people's Kazan will be restored to the family of Soviet Russia.

Down with the Czechoslovak, Anglo-French, Japanese and other bandits!

Death to the White Guards!

Destruction to the traitorous bourgeois of Kazan!

Long live Workers' and Peasants' Soviet Russia!

EXAM-STYLE QUESTION

AO3

SKILLS ANALYSIS, ADAPTIVE LEARNING, CREATIVITY

Study Sources K and L.
How far does Source K support Source L about the message the Reds gave to people in areas captured by the Whites?
Explain your answer. **(8 marks)**

HINT

Don't forget that this question asks 'how far', so you are expected to find points of agreement and points of difference.

RECAP

RECALL QUESTIONS

1 Lenin's government was known as Sovnarkom for short. What was the full name of this government (in English)?
2 What did the Decree on Land abolish?
3 Which party received the most votes in the Constituent Assembly elections, in November 1917?
4 Which foreign power had given the Bolsheviks money and allowed Lenin to travel back to Russia in 1917, hoping that he would pull Russia out of the First World War?
5 The Bolsheviks renamed the Russian Republic as Russia on 25 October 1917. What does RSFSR stand for?
6 Why did signing the Treaty of Brest-Litovsk make the Bolsheviks unpopular?
7 What government position did Trotsky hold during the Civil War (from March 1918)?
8 Which one of the following was a White leader who attacked the Bolsheviks from Estonia?
   a Kolchak   b Yudenich   c Denikin   d Wrangel
9 Which foreign force took control of large sections of the Trans-Siberian Railway during the Civil War?
10 What key event took place on 17 July 1918?

CHECKPOINT

STRENGTHEN
S1 Identify two problems facing the Bolsheviks as they tried to strengthen their control after October 1917.
S2 Russia gave up high percentages of its coal mines, industry, railways, farmland and population in return for peace with Germany and its allies in the Treaty of Brest-Litovsk. List what you think these percentages were, from memory. Check your answers as a class.
S3 Identify three Red strengths and three White weaknesses that help explain the Bolshevik victory in the Civil War.

CHALLENGE
C1 Design a 'Red' poster to encourage peasants to join the Red Army against the Whites. You could look online for examples of real Bolshevik Civil War propaganda.
C2 Lenin once said, 'It is facts that are important, not words.' Do you agree with the belief that it is what politicians do when they get into power that matters, not what they say in order to get into power in the first place? Discuss this in a group or debate it as a class.
C3 'The Bolsheviks were foolish to agree to such bad terms in the Treaty of Brest-Litovsk. They should have negotiated better terms.' How far do you agree with this statement? Explain your answer.

SUMMARY

- Elections were held for the Constituent Assembly in November 1917.
- Throughout November and December, the Bolsheviks introduced a series of decrees to bring 'Peace, Land and Bread' to the Russian people.
- The Constituent Assembly was dissolved on its first day.
- The Treaty of Brest-Litovsk took Russia out of the First World War.
- The Reds and Whites (and Greens) fought a Civil War.
- Other countries sent troops to fight against the Bolsheviks.
- The royal family was executed at Yekaterinburg.
- Lenin introduced War Communism and the Red Terror.
- In 1920, the Reds won the Civil War.

EXAM GUIDANCE: PART (C) QUESTIONS

Study Extract C.

SOURCE A

From a letter written to her family, by an American visitor to Russia in 1924. She is explaining her views on the new communist government.

Russia is such a strange mixture. I can't generalize about it, because one thing contradicts another. On the one hand there is the cruelty, even now, to the counter-revolutionaries. But it is not fair to dwell on that because both sides were cruel in the civil war, the Bolsheviks more so only because they came out on top. Everyone here assumes that if the Whites had won they would have exterminated the Reds so far as they could catch them. And I have been told by Whites that in the matter of brutality, of killing prisoners, and hostages, of torturing and the rest, there was nothing to choose between the two sides. One woman who was a Red Cross nurse, said that she blamed the Whites more, because they were upper class people and one expected more of them than the lower class Reds.

SOURCE B

From the diary of Colonel Drozdovsky, a White General. He wrote this account in March 1918.

We arrived at Vladimirovka about 5.00 p.m. Having surrounded the village we placed the machine guns in position, fired a couple of volleys in the direction of the village, and everybody there took cover. Then our mounted troops entered the village and put the members of the Bolshevik committee to death. After the executions, the houses of the culprits were burned and the whole male population under forty-five whipped soundly, the whipping being done by the old men. Then the population was ordered to deliver without pay the best cattle, pigs, fowl, hay and bread for our men, as well as the best horses.

EXTRACT C

From a history of the modern world, written in 2001.

Some White leaders were brutal and established a harsh rule over their territories. The 'White Terror' encouraged many Russians to support the Reds. But Bolshevik victory also came as a result of their ruthlessness. Many Russians supported the Reds through fear and the civil war had a disastrous effect on a population already devastated by war. There was a serious famine in 1921 and it is estimated that about 5 million Russians starved to death.

AO3   **AO4**

SKILLS ▷ CRITICAL THINKING, REASONING, DECISION MAKING, ADAPTIVE LEARNING, CREATIVITY, INNOVATION

Question to be answered: Extract C suggests that one of the reasons why the Bolsheviks won the civil war was because of brutality by the Whites.

How far do you agree with this interpretation?

Use Extract C, Sources A and B and your own knowledge to explain your answer. (16 marks)

Analysis Question: What do I have to do to answer this question well?

■ You have to demonstrate that you can use two sources and your own knowledge in order to show how far you agree with a historian's interpretation of an event.

■ Obviously, the starting point is the interpretation. Read the extract and see what evidence the author uses to support his/her interpretation. Only when you know this can you look at contemporary sources to see if they agree or disagree.

■ Do not be tempted to write all you know about the topic. You need to select those parts of your own knowledge that are directly relevant to the interpretation given in the question.

The plan for your answer could look like this.

Paragraph 1: show how the first source supports and disagrees with the interpretation, and use own knowledge to support this evaluation.

Paragraph 2: show how the second source supports and disagrees with the interpretation and use own knowledge to support this evaluation.

Paragraph 3: reach an overall judgement that is supported by brief references to the most important points made in paragraphs 1 and 2.

Answer

I agree with this interpretation because there is evidence in Source A to support it. Source A supports the view that the Whites were brutal because it says that if they had won they would have exterminated the Bolsheviks. It also said a Red Cross nurse condemned the Whites for their behaviour because they were upper class and should have behaved better. Source B completely supports the idea that the Whites lost because they were brutal. Who is going to support a side that slaughters men and steals all the grain and livestock? The extract itself says there was a White Terror.

But some of the evidence contradicts that the Reds won because people hated the brutality of the Whites. According to Source A, cruelty was still being committed by the Reds in 1924 and the Bolsheviks were even more cruel than the Whites. The extract says the Reds were ruthless and people supported them out of fear. Source B doesn't actually contradict the interpretation, but you can probably say that the Bolsheviks would have done the same to the Whites.

So I don't really agree.

What are the strengths of this answer?
- *A sound understanding is shown of the two sources.*
- *The two sources are clearly linked to different areas of the interpretation, and agreements and disagreements are identified.*

What are the weaknesses?
- *Although the question clearly states 'use your own knowledge', contextual knowledge is not used in support of the points made.*
- *The answer looks at the arguments for and against the interpretation using the two sources and the extract itself, but it does not answer the question 'how far?'.*
- *To get the very highest marks, the answer has to do more than say 'yes and no'. It has to consider the strength of the argument on each side.*

Answer checklist
☐ Identifies agreement and disagreement with the hypothesis
☐ Uses information from the two sources, the extract and own contextual knowledge
☐ Addresses 'how far?' by 'weighing' the evidence to see which side is most strongly supported.

5. WAR COMMUNISM AND THE NEW ECONOMIC POLICY (NEP)

LEARNING OBJECTIVES

- Understand the reasons for, nature and effects of War Communism
- Understand the reasons for, nature and effects of the New Economic Policy
- Understand the achievements of Lenin to 1924.

War Communism was a system Lenin introduced to put the state in control of industry and agriculture. Under this system, the Bolsheviks could take supplies as and when they needed from peasants and workers for the Red Army, which helped them win the Civil War. However, War Communism had a terrible effect on the Russian people. In the countryside, millions of peasants starved because their crops had been taken away from them. In the cities, workers faced such harsh discipline and such desperate food shortages that many felt they had been better off under tsarism. When the previously highly loyal sailors at the Kronstadt naval base mutinied, something had to be done. Lenin brought in the New Economic Policy, which was a step back from communism and re-introduced some capitalism into the economy. The NEP reduced unrest in the country, though some in the Bolshevik Party thought Lenin had betrayed communism.

5.1 WAR COMMUNISM

LEARNING OBJECTIVES

■ Understand features of War Communism

■ Understand reasons why War Communism was introduced

■ Understand the effects of War Communism.

In order to win the Civil War, the Bolsheviks put the state in control of the economy. Instead of private business owners deciding what to make, the state decided what to produce; instead of private farmers deciding how much of their crops to sell, the state decided how much was needed to come from farmers. The state also decided how the supplies would be divided and shared, which meant the Bolsheviks could make sure the Red Army had what it needed to win the war. This system was called War Communism. It was introduced in June 1918 and lasted until March 1921.

FEATURES OF WAR COMMUNISM

Lenin introduced War Communism so that the Russian economy could meet the needs of the military and industrial workers. However, this meant huge sacrifices for everyone else, and the system also went against some of the decrees of October 1917, as shown by the following examples.

■ Under War Communism, peasants were not allowed to sell their crops. The state requisitioned the crops and left the peasants a small amount for their own needs. The consequence was that peasants often ended up hiding the grain they grew, even though anyone suspected of hoarding grain would be shot.

■ Food rationing began in cities, with soldiers and workers getting more food than others.

■ A new **central planning** organisation called the Supreme Economic Council (Russian name *Vesenkha*) was introduced in December 1917. It decided what the economy needed and set targets. Workers' soviets no longer made the decisions for their factories.

■ Factories with more than 10 workers were nationalised and given production targets by the government.

■ Workers were put under government control. Strikes were banned in order to guarantee production targets. Everyone old enough to work was forced to work – a policy called labour **conscription**. Workers could be moved from one city to another to work.

KEY TERMS

central planning when the state controls the economy and decides what is to be produced and how it is to be distributed

conscription when people have to carry out some sort of service for the state, for example, military service

EXAM-STYLE QUESTION

A01

Describe **two** features of War Communism.   **(6 marks)**

HINT

Remember to make it obvious to the examiner that you are covering two features. A good way to do this is to have two paragraphs: the first one should start with 'One feature is…', and the second one should start with 'Another feature is…'.

REASONS FOR WAR COMMUNISM

Lenin introduced War Communism because the Red Army had to be supplied with food, clothing and weapons if the Bolsheviks were going to win the Civil War. The Bolsheviks therefore needed factories and farms to be run more efficiently, and needed the workers to work harder.

STATE CONTROL OF INDUSTRY

When the Bolsheviks took control of Russia in 1917, the economy was in a very bad condition. Industries were producing only 60 per cent of what they had produced in 1913. The transport network was disrupted and raw materials were not getting to the factories. The banks were not lending money to factories after the Bolshevik revolution. The Bolsheviks had also lost 40 per cent of the industrial areas of the old Russian empire following the Treaty of Brest-Litovsk. Workforce numbers were also going down: food shortages meant workers were leaving the starving cities and going back to their family villages to find food.

The Bolsheviks used central planning and strict controls on the factories and their workers to try to deal with this problem. Central planning decided what each nationalised factory should produce and organised the supply of raw materials. At first the Bolsheviks tried to use persuasion and propaganda to make the workers work harder, but when this failed they brought in strict discipline. From 1919, workers could be moved from one sector of work to another, and were then forbidden to leave that sector. From 1920, anyone of working age (between 16 and 50) could be made to work for the state: on building sites, in farming, on the railways, clearing snow from the roads.

Ultimately, the Civil War proved to be a very difficult time for workers. While some of them were well fed, most were not – and everyone worked under harsh conditions in order to meet the state's targets.

STATE CONTROL OF FOOD SUPPLY

Food shortages in the cities increased after 1917. One reason was the loss of so much farmland to Germany from the Treaty of Brest-Litovsk. Another reason was that the Whites were controlling a number of important farming areas.

Generally, peasants in the countryside had enough land to feed themselves, but they were not growing enough food to supply the cities and the Red Army – partly because the cities were not making enough products that peasants wanted to buy. Why would peasants work harder to grow more food to sell, if there was nothing to buy with the money they would earn?

War Communism used requisitioning to try and deal with this problem. The state decided how much of their crops peasants should be allowed to keep to live on, and took the rest. The Bolsheviks promised compensation to the peasants in the future. The state then redistributed the crops to the Red Army and the city workers. This was successful in increasing food supply. In 1918, the state was collecting less than 1 million tonnes of grain from the peasants in a year; by 1920 this had risen to 6 million tonnes. Still, this was still not enough to feed the Russian population.

A Bolshevik poster from 1919. It reads: 'You shed your blood for the workers' and peasants' revolution. The workers and peasants are giving up all they have for you, their last clothes and boots. Take them!'

KEY TERM

ideological connected to particular ideas or a set of beliefs, for example, the Bolsheviks were committed to Marxist ideology – the theories of Karl Marx

IDEOLOGICAL REASONS

There were **ideological** reasons for introducing War Communism, too. The Bolsheviks thought the system was close to how they believed a communist country should be run: with the state in control of all production and without individuals making any profit from buying and selling.

Some historians say that the Civil War gave the Bolsheviks an excuse for rapidly moving towards a communist economy. Central planning of the economy and state control of industry and agriculture were all elements of a communist system. War Communism also saw the Bolsheviks replacing money with tokens, which workers exchanged for food and clothing. Socialist thinkers had predicted that communist societies would have no need for money. Other historians say that War Communism had more to do with the Bolsheviks bringing in emergency measures to deal with a desperate situation, rather than ideological reasons.

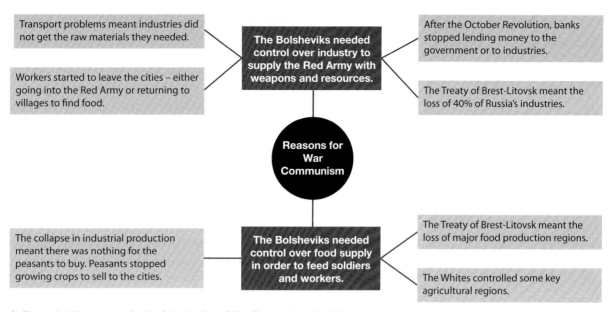

Transport problems meant industries did not get the raw materials they needed.

Workers started to leave the cities – either going into the Red Army or returning to villages to find food.

The Bolsheviks needed control over industry to supply the Red Army with weapons and resources.

After the October Revolution, banks stopped lending money to the government or to industries.

The Treaty of Brest-Litovsk meant the loss of 40% of Russia's industries.

Reasons for War Communism

The collapse in industrial production meant there was nothing for the peasants to buy. Peasants stopped growing crops to sell to the cities.

The Bolsheviks needed control over food supply in order to feed soldiers and workers.

The Treaty of Brest-Litovsk meant the loss of major food production regions.

The Whites controlled some key agricultural regions.

▲ Figure 5.1 Key reasons for the introduction of War Communism in 1918

ACTIVITY

1 Figure 5.1 shows some reasons for War Communism. Study the diagram and decide which three you think are the most important. Justify your decisions.

2 Imagine you are a worker who had supported the Bolsheviks during the October Revolution. How would you be feeling during the Civil War?

  a Who do you blame for the food shortages in Russia: the Bolsheviks, or the Whites who seized control of farming regions?

  b Do you agree that work conditions need to be strict to win the war for the Reds, or do you now blame the Bolsheviks for going back on their promises to the working class?

3 Study Source A. Design a 'White' propaganda poster that gives a different perspective on the Reds' food requisition, for example, telling peasants that the Reds' use of force to take grain from them is a bad idea.

EFFECTS OF WAR COMMUNISM

War Communism was effective in making sure that the Red Army had what it needed to win the Civil War. However, it was unpopular with peasants and workers alike. It was also considered an economic disaster.

EFFECTS ON THE PEASANTS

Requisitioning turned the peasants against the Bolsheviks. The requisitioning brigades had taken so much from the peasants that they were left with very little to eat – sometimes not even the seeds to plant the next year's harvest. The amount of crops grown in the country declined as a result: by 1920, farm production had fallen to 37 per cent of what it had been in 1913, before the war and revolutions. Food shortages increased in the countryside; in some areas these shortages became famines.

Faced with peasants who often hid their grain stores, the requisitioning brigades began using increasing levels of violence to meet their requisitioning targets. Thousands of people were killed in these conflicts, which grew into whole-region revolts in some cases. To avoid having their farm animals requisitioned, many peasants decided to kill them – even though this meant the peasants would no longer have animals with which to pull their ploughs and carts.

It is true, however, that peasants in general still preferred the Reds to the Whites, as the Whites would have returned all seized land to the original owners.

KULAKS AND BOLSHEVIK IDEOLOGY

To justify the conflicts happening in the countryside, the Bolsheviks blamed the unrest on the rich peasants who were resisting the requisitioning brigades; they used the term *kulak* for these rich peasants, meaning 'closed fist' – a tightly closed hand that refuses to release what it is grasping. The *kulaks* were seen as counter-revolutionary capitalists, whereas the rest of the peasants, especially the poorest ones, were seen as supporters of the revolution. This theory had a significant effect on how the Bolsheviks dealt with the peasants.

SOURCE B

From a secret order sent by Lenin to the commissars in Penza, a region of Russia that was experiencing peasant revolts in August 1918.

We need to set an example. You need to hang – hang without fail, and do it so that the public sees – at least 100 notorious kulaks, the rich and the bloodsuckers. Publish their names. Take away all of their grain. Execute the hostages…

This needs to be accomplished in such a way that people for hundreds of miles around will see, tremble, know and scream out: let's choke and strangle those blood-sucking kulaks.

ACTIVITY

Study Source B. How far does what it says affect your judgement of Lenin? Explain your answer.

EFFECTS ON THE WORKERS

Although War Communism did help to make sure the Red Army had the supplies it needed, the same could not be said for most workers in the cities. Food became so hard to find that huge numbers of workers left the cities to return to their family villages. Between 1918 and 1920, half of Moscow's population went back to the countryside. In Petrograd, almost three quarters of the city's population disappeared in the same way.

Across the country, the number of people working in factories fell by one half, and production halved as well. Industries that were still working were now almost all producing supplies for the Red Army, making virtually no products for ordinary people in the cities or in the countryside.

As the state was not providing the people with what they needed, everyone used the illegal **black market** to get what they needed to survive. It is estimated that the black market supplied 70 per cent of the food that people ate under War Communism. Black market prices were very high, however, which made life harder for the workers.

While the Civil War was still being fought, the Bolsheviks were generally successful in convincing workers that the Whites and foreign invaders were to blame for the desperately hard living and working conditions. But once the Reds had won the war, protests against the harsh conditions increased rapidly.

SOURCE C

A photo of starving children taken in October 1921, when famines caused by crop failures, the civil war and War Communism hit large areas of the Soviet Union.

5.2 THE KRONSTADT NAVAL MUTINY

THE KRONSTADT NAVAL BASE

The sailors of the Kronstadt naval base had been strong supporters of revolution in Russia. Kronstadt was a very important naval base, as it guarded Petrograd. During the February Revolution in 1917, Kronstadt sailors rioted and murdered many of their tsarist officers. They set up a Kronstadt soviet, took part in the July Days, and joined the Red Guard in defending Petrograd from Kornilov in August, and then again in seizing power from the Provisional Government in October. In January 1918, Kronstadt sailors were among the troops used by Lenin to shut down the Constituent Assembly. In short, the sailors from the Kronstadt base had been heroes of the revolution in 1917. Trotsky called them the 'reddest of the red'.

Despite this, on 28 February 1921, there was a mutiny of Kronstadt sailors on the battleship *Petropavlovsk*. This quickly spread to the whole base; more than 15,000 sailors mutinied.

REASONS FOR THE MUTINY

KEY TERM

bureaucrat someone who works in a bureaucracy and uses official rules very strictly

There was growing opposition to the difficulties created by War Communism amongst workers, especially after the bread ration was cut again in January 1921. Workers began to strike in Moscow and Petrograd, protesting about food shortages and lack of freedom. There was increasing anger about the way that Bolshevik **bureaucrats** had more food than the workers, and enjoyed many party advantages, such as comfortable homes to live in. Many of the Kronstadt sailors shared the workers' anger. They were especially furious that the Bolsheviks were betraying their socialist revolution by imprisoning and executing people without trial.

SOURCE D

From an anti-Bolshevik statement by the socialist workers of the Nevsky District, in Petrograd.

We know who is afraid of the Constituent Assembly. It is they who will no longer be able to rob the people. Instead they will have to answer before the representatives of the people for their deceit, their robberies, and their crimes.

Down with the hated Communists!

Down with the Soviet Government!

Long live the Constituent Assembly!

SOURCE E

Extracts from the demands of the Kronstadt sailors, 1921.

- *To re-elect the soviets immediately by secret voting because the soviets now do not represent the will of the workers and peasants [because they are now controlled by Bolsheviks].*

- *Freedom of speech for workers, peasants, anarchists and socialist parties.*

- *All political prisoners from socialist parties to be released, as well as all workers, peasants, soldiers and sailors who have been imprisoned for taking part in [anti-Bolshevik] working-class and peasant movements.*

- *All workers to have equal rations.*

- *To grant peasants the full right to do what they think best with their own land.*

ACTIVITY

1 What do you think Trotsky meant when he called the Kronstadt sailors the 'reddest of the red'?

2 Match the Kronstadt demands in Source E to the following explanations.

   a There was anger that some Bolshevik bureaucrats got more food and better living conditions than workers.

   b The Bolsheviks had banned any other political parties.

   c The soviets were under Bolshevik control and forced to vote the way the government wanted them to.

   d Bolshevik food requisitioning took all the spare crops from peasant farmers.

   e The Cheka had arrested and imprisoned (or executed) those it suspected of acting against the Bolsheviks.

SOURCE F

From the *Kronstadt Izvestia*, a newspaper published by the Kronstadt sailors during the mutiny. This extract is taken from the last issue, published on 16 March 1921.

The Bolsheviks carried out nationalization of the plants and factories. From a slave of the capitalist, the worker became a slave of the bureaucratic institutions.

The entire labouring peasantry was counted with the kulaks, declared an enemy of the people... In exchange for grain requisitioned, and cows and horses taken away, there were Cheka raids and executions...

Any free thought, any fair criticism of the actions of the criminal rulers was made a crime, punishable by imprisonment, and not rarely even by execution.

EXAM-STYLE QUESTION

A03

SKILLS ANALYSIS, ADAPTIVE LEARNING, CREATIVITY

Study Sources E and F.
How far does Source F support the evidence of Source E about why the Kronstadt sailors opposed the Bolsheviks?
Explain your answer.   **(8 marks)**

HINT

Remember, when answering a 'how far' question, you need to show the ways in which one source does and does not support the other.

THE REACTION OF THE BOLSHEVIK LEADERSHIP

Although Lenin and other senior Bolsheviks were shocked that the Kronstadt naval base had joined in the protests against the government, they did not hesitate to use violence to put down the mutiny. Trotsky organised a huge force of 50,000 Red Army soldiers to storm the naval base while it was still possible to attack across the ice of the frozen Gulf of Finland. There was fierce fighting and it took until 17 March for the base to be under government control again. Around 8000 sailors escaped across the ice to Finland. Prisoners were handed over to the Cheka, and around 500 sailors were executed for rebelling against the government.

SOURCE G

Red Army soldiers during the battle to retake the Kronstadt naval base in March 1921.

THE SIGNIFICANCE OF THE KRONSTADT NAVAL MUTINY

By 1921, the Bolsheviks were facing significant opposition in the countryside from widespread peasant unrest. The growth in opposition in the cities was very worrying, especially when it involved workers, soldiers and sailors who should have been Bolshevik supporters. Lenin recognised that War Communism was putting his control over the country at risk. It was time to make changes to reduce the pressures on the Russian people. So, Lenin abandoned War Communism and turned to a new policy that would bring back elements of capitalism.

5.3 THE NEW ECONOMIC POLICY

LEARNING OBJECTIVES

- Understand the reasons why the NEP was introduced
- Understand key features of the NEP
- Understand the effects of the NEP.

ECONOMIC CRISIS

The Bolsheviks had won the Civil War in 1921, but the country was in ruins. The economy was barely functioning. It had become a daily struggle for people to find enough to eat, both in the cities and in the countryside. Peasant farming could not produce enough food to feed the country, even with the requisitioning brigades taking everything that villages had. Crop failures in 1920 added to the crisis: between 1920 and 1921, famines in the Volga region alone affected 20 million people, with an estimated 5 million dying from starvation and disease.

SOURCE H

Agricultural and industrial production figures in Russia in 1913 and 1921.

	▼ 1913	▼ 1921
Grain harvest	80.1 million tonnes	46.1 million tonnes
Factory production	10.2 million roubles	2 million roubles
Steel production	4.231 million tonnes	183,000 tonnes
Rail freight carried	132 million tonnes	39 million tonnes

SOURCE I

From a diary written in 1920 by a Petrograd professor, describing a typical day.

3 December 1920

Today I got up at 9 a.m. There is no point getting up before since it is dark and the house lights are not working. There is a shortage of fuel... I drank some coffee (made from oats) without milk or sugar, of course, and ate a piece of bread from a loaf bought two weeks ago for 1,500 roubles... At the Nikolaev Bridge I finally caught up with a No. 4 tram. There was no current on the line and the tram was stationary. I still don't understand this. All the trams had stopped but why had they started out if they knew there was not enough fuel to complete their journeys? ... I stayed for half an hour and then went to the University, where there was supposed to be a ration of cabbage handed out at 3 p.m. ... But again I was out of luck: it turned out that the cabbage had not been delivered and would be given out tomorrow. And not to professors but only to students.

ACTIVITY

Using Sources H and I, plus your own knowledge, explain why life in 1920 was so difficult for:
- peasants in the countryside
- workers in the cities
- former middle-class and upper-class people.

POLITICAL CRISIS

At the same time, Bolsheviks also faced a political crisis. Once the Civil War was won, the Bolsheviks could no longer continue to blame the Whites for causing all the terrible suffering. In the cities, workers began protesting again, against the harsh discipline in the factories. By the end of 1920, three quarters of Petrograd factories were on strike. In the countryside, peasant unrest against food requisitioning turned whole regions, for example, the Tambov region, into areas that the Bolsheviks could not enter. Even within the Bolshevik Party, some members began calling for a relaxation of the harsh discipline in the factories, where workers could be imprisoned or executed for missing production targets.

LENIN'S U-TURN

When the Kronstadt Mutiny happened in 1921, Lenin called it 'the flash which lit up reality, better than anything else'. Although Lenin had hoped that War Communism would help the Bolsheviks build a communist state, the Kronstadt Mutiny forced him to recognise that the system was destroying any trust that the workers and (especially) peasants had in the Bolsheviks and in **communism**. At the 10th Party Congress in March 1921, Lenin made it clear that the revolution could not succeed unless the government took very urgent steps to give the peasants what they wanted.

KEY TERM

communism a system of government in which all property is owned by the community, and in which each person contributes and receives according to his or her ability and needs

SOURCE J

From a pamphlet written by Lenin in April 1921.

[In] war communism we actually took from the peasant all his surpluses – and sometimes even a part of his necessaries – to meet the requirements of the army and sustain the workers…

The political situation in the spring of 1921 was such that immediate, very resolute and urgent measures had to be taken to improve the condition of the peasants and to increase their productive forces.

Why the peasants and not the workers?

Because you need grain and fuel to improve the condition of the workers.

KEY FEATURES OF THE NEW ECONOMIC POLICY

The New Economic Policy (NEP) reversed the economic changes forced on the country by War Communism in the following ways.
- The free market was reintroduced. Now peasants could sell their produce and decide what price to sell it at. They paid a 10 per cent tax on any produce they sold.
- Grain requisition was ended.

- Although the state kept control of big factories, any banks and businesses with fewer than 20 workers could again be privately owned and run to make a profit.
- Foreign experts were brought in to improve how factories were run. Between 1920 and 1925, 20,000 experts came from the USA and Canada. These experts were paid more than ordinary workers.
- Any Russians could open a shop and sell or hire goods for a profit. Those who did so became known as 'Nepmen'.

ACTIVITY

1 What is a U-turn? Why was it a U-turn for Lenin to argue that the Bolsheviks should prioritise giving the peasants what they needed?
2 Working in groups, identify what the NEP changed in order to improve life for the peasants.

EFFECTS OF THE NEW ECONOMIC POLICY

KEY TERM

Soviet Union from December 1922, the Russian Soviet Socialist Republic (RSFSR) and the other soviet socialist republics formed the Union of Soviet Socialist Republics (USSR) – Soviet Union for short

ECONOMIC EFFECTS

The NEP had four main effects on the economy of the **Soviet Union**.

- Agricultural production increased rapidly – peasants grew a lot more food. This was because peasants were now able to sell any surplus for a profit. Each peasant farmer still had to produce a fixed amount of their crops for the government (called a tax in kind) but they were allowed to sell anything left over. By 1923, many peasants were paying tax in cash instead of in grain, which made them eager to earn more money.
- As production increased, so did supplies of food. Under War Communism, only the state bought and sold products. The NEP allowed people to trade again, so peasants and traders started to move food crops to sell in the towns and cities. A new currency, the *chervonets*, was introduced in 1922. Rationing was abolished: people now had to buy food with their own money. Again, this made people eager to earn more money.
- Industrial growth also increased, especially for smaller businesses that were now privately owned and run for profit. There was a lot of demand in the countryside for simple manufactured products like clothes and shoes. Many traders went directly from the factories to the countryside to sell these manufactured products.
- Some foreign governments thought the introduction of the NEP meant that the Soviet Union's experiment with communism was over. A number of countries were eager to encourage the Soviet Union's return to capitalism: Britain, for example, made trade deals with the Soviet Union, which helped boost the latter's finances.

SOURCE K

Agricultural and industrial production figures in Russia in 1913, 1921 and 1923.

	▼ 1913	▼ 1921	▼ 1923
Grain harvest	80.1 million tonnes	46.1 million tonnes	56.6 million tonnes
Factory production	10.2 million roubles	2 million roubles	4.6 million roubles
Steel production	4.231 million tonnes	183,000 tonnes	709,000 tonnes
Rail freight carried	132 million tonnes	39 million tonnes	58 million tonnes

ACTIVITY

Draw a bar graph of the data in Source K. Annotate your graph to explain the economic changes between War Communism and the first 2 years of the NEP.

THE 'SCISSORS CRISIS'

By 1923, so much food was being produced that food prices in the cities and towns started to go down. However, industrial production was developing at a slower rate, and there were still shortages of manufactured products. This meant that prices for the manufactured products stayed high.

In the short term, this situation made the peasants less eager to sell their crops because they were getting less money for them, and then they would have had to spend a bigger share of that money on manufactured products. The government was very concerned that there would soon not be enough grain from peasant farmers to feed people in the cities. Trotsky called this the 'scissors crisis' because a graph comparing industrial prices (which went up) and prices for farm products (which went down) looked like an open pair of scissors. The government took steps to lower industrial prices, which helped to reduce the problem.

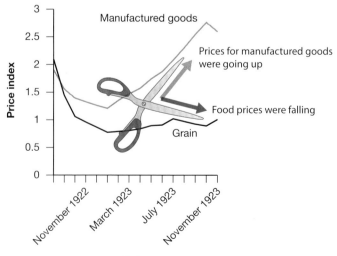

▶ Figure 5.2 The scissors crisis, 1923

SOCIAL EFFECTS

The NEP was good for the peasants, especially those with the most land since they could grow the most surplus and earn the most money. Gradually, the peasant revolts ended, although this was partly the result of the discontented regions being overwhelmed by the Red Army, which stamped out the unrest. Thanks to the NEP, the peasants were generally happy to tolerate the government, although many remained cautious about what it might do next.

Life in the cities and towns recovered also: shops opened, as did restaurants and cafes, banks, hotels, theatres and other types of entertainment. A new social group called Nepmen appeared. Nepmen were traders who had made profits from the shortages of food and manufactured products, travelling around to sell what they had where prices were highest. Although the NEP had saved the Bolsheviks from ruin, it also led to a growth in **inequality** in the Soviet Union. This was not what socialism was supposed to achieve.

OPPOSITION TO THE NEP

SOURCE L

This Russian drawing from 1920 is called *NEPmen*.

At first, most Bolsheviks were prepared to go along with the NEP. This was because the economic and political crisis in 1921 was so bad that there did not seem to be any other alternative. Lenin and the other senior Bolsheviks also told the party that the NEP was only going to be a very short-term measure: Lenin said it was a case of taking one step backwards in order to take a leap forwards towards communism, and described the policy as a 'peasant Brest-Litovsk', that is, a deeply unpleasant and painful thing to do but something that would quickly produce great benefits for the Soviet Union. Lenin is also reported to have threatened to resign as leader if the party voted against the NEP.

However, the policy was deeply worrying for many Bolsheviks for a number of reasons:

- War Communism, although painful, was clearly in line with communist theory: with state control of industry and agriculture, and an end to banks, private trade and money.
- The NEP, although successful, looked like a return to capitalism, with some people getting very rich while the rest remained poor.
- Instead of prioritising workers and keeping food prices for them low, the NEP favoured the peasants and let them charge the highest price they could get for their crops.
- The NEP was making the most successful peasant farmers far richer than the rest of the peasant population. At the same time, living conditions for factory workers were hardly improving at all. Despite the efforts to wipe out the bourgeoisie and kulaks during War Communism, the NEP seemed to be re-creating new classes of rich and poor in both the countryside and in the cities.

ACTIVITY

Study Source L. Would you say the artist approved of the *Nepmen*? Explain your answer.

SOURCE M

From a book written by a leading Bolshevik in 1937.

In just a few years, the NEP restored to Soviet Union an aspect of prosperity. But to many of us this prosperity was sometimes distasteful... There was gambling, drunkenness and all the old filth of former times... Classes were reborn in front of our eyes... There was a growing gap between the prosperity of the few and the misery of the many.

SOURCE N

From a letter by a member of the Young Communist League to the Central Committee of the Communist Party of the Soviet Union, written in August 1926.

I reckon it's time to pay the maximum amount of attention to this question, the question of abolishing NEP, because it is horrible to see here in this Soviet state people so fat they can't get through a door, but mainly because it's time to stop this shameless cheating and the existence of people living off the labour of workers and peasants... I really don't think this NEP is any real use to us as a Soviet state; admittedly, it was useful once, but now it's harmful...

EXAM-STYLE QUESTION

AO3

SKILLS ANALYSIS, ADAPTIVE LEARNING, CREATIVITY

Study Sources M and N.
How far does Source N support the evidence of Source M about reasons for opposition to the NEP?
Explain your answer.   **(8 marks)**

HINT

Take care to use only the relevant information in the sources. When you provide detail from a source, make sure you are doing so to be able to compare it with what the other source says.

ACTIVITY

Do you think the author of Extract A supported the NEP? Explain your answer.

EXTRACT A

From *A People's Tragedy*, published in 1996.

[A deep] ... resentment – of the 'Nepmen'... and the 'kulaks' – remained deeply buried in the hearts of many people, especially the... workers and the party rank and file [ordinary Party members] ... [the] Soviet Union in the 1920s remained a society at war with itself – full of unresolved social tensions and resentments just beneath the surface. In this sense the deepest legacy of the revolution was its failure to eliminate the social inequalities that had brought it about in the first place.

5.4 ACHIEVEMENTS OF LENIN TO 1924

LEARNING OBJECTIVES

■ Understand reactions to Lenin's death in 1924

■ Understand Lenin's achievements to 1924

■ Evaluate the significance of Lenin's achievements.

LENIN'S ILLNESS AND DEATH

Lenin died in 1924, at the age of 53. He had been ill for the previous 2 years, having suffered a stroke in May 1922. He had a second stroke in December 1922, after which he retired from the party leadership and politics. In March 1923, he had a third stroke, which left him unable to speak. He suffered great pain until his death on 21 January 1924. The stresses of leadership, his **workaholic** personality (he regularly worked 14 hours a day) and his injuries from Fanya Kaplan's assassination attempt back in 1918 probably all contributed to his early death.

When he was alive, Lenin was already seen as a sort of saint by some people in the Soviet Union. After his death, the 'cult' or worship of Lenin increased greatly. Lenin's words were treated like a sacred text and his image was everywhere. Petrograd was renamed Leningrad in his honour. One common slogan in the Soviet Union was 'Lenin is with us', which continued to guide the Communist Party long after his death.

SOURCE O

A crowd at Lenin's funeral in January 1924.

EXTEND YOUR KNOWLEDGE

LENIN ON DISPLAY
Lenin's body was embalmed after his death and was put on display. In the first 6 weeks after his death, 100,000 people visited his tomb and viewed his preserved body. It is still on display today; tens of millions of people have visited it since Lenin's death.

LENIN'S ACHIEVEMENTS

When the Bolsheviks took power from the Provisional Government in October 1917, most people were sure that they would last only a few weeks. Other socialist revolutionary parties did not support the way the Bolsheviks had taken control. There were so many enemies to overcome, not just within the Soviet Union but internationally. Yet, despite a civil war and devastating economic and social problems, the Bolsheviks held on to power. They won the Civil War and by 1924 were fully in control of the Soviet Union. Lenin was certainly vitally important in planning and organising this success.

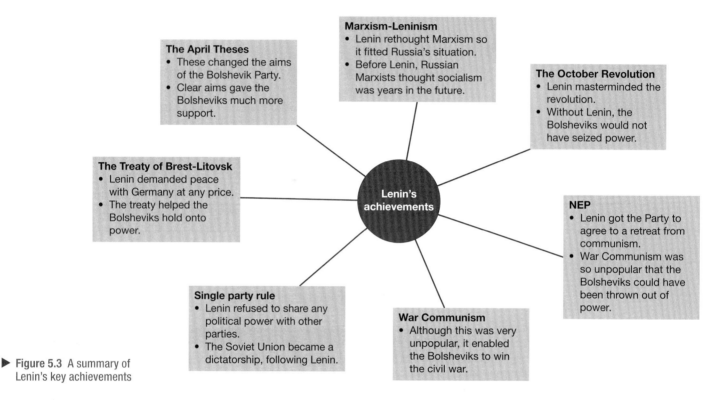

The April Theses
- These changed the aims of the Bolshevik Party.
- Clear aims gave the Bolsheviks much more support.

Marxism-Leninism
- Lenin rethought Marxism so it fitted Russia's situation.
- Before Lenin, Russian Marxists thought socialism was years in the future.

The October Revolution
- Lenin masterminded the revolution.
- Without Lenin, the Bolsheviks would not have seized power.

The Treaty of Brest-Litovsk
- Lenin demanded peace with Germany at any price.
- The treaty helped the Bolsheviks hold onto power.

Lenin's achievements

NEP
- Lenin got the Party to agree to a retreat from communism.
- War Communism was so unpopular that the Bolsheviks could have been thrown out of power.

Single party rule
- Lenin refused to share any political power with other parties.
- The Soviet Union became a dictatorship, following Lenin.

War Communism
- Although this was very unpopular, it enabled the Bolsheviks to win the civil war.

▶ **Figure 5.3** A summary of Lenin's key achievements

Lenin was the founder of the Bolshevik Party, it was his leadership of the Party that created the conditions for its rapid increase in popularity, he led the Party in its seizure of power in Russia in October 1917, and it was Lenin who then went on to be the first head of the new Soviet state, which became the Soviet Union in 1922. His political theories set out the principles of how the Bolsheviks would rule. Lenin was at the centre of the Red victory in the Civil War, of the development of War Communism and of the New Economic Policy. It was not always easy for Lenin to persuade the Bolshevik Party to support his ideas, but one way or another, by argument or by threats of resignation, he convinced people to follow his leadership. After his death, there was a leadership struggle to see who should replace him. But there was never any doubt that whoever the new leader was, the Soviet Union would continue to be a communist country. That shows just how much Lenin achieved.

There are many different interpretations of Lenin and his achievements. For example:

Lenin was the main reason for a second, socialist revolution in Russia in 1917 – without him, the revolution would not have happened.

There were many different social, economic and political pressures on the Provisional Government in 1917. Lenin's achievement was simply to recognise that it would be easy to seize power.

Lenin truly believed that socialism would provide a way to help the workers and peasants in the Soviet Union. Everything he did was focused on protecting socialism.

Lenin wanted power at all costs. Everything he did was focused on making sure that only his party had power.

KEY TERM

obituary an article in a newspaper about the life of someone who has just died

ACTIVITY

1 Study the diagram of Lenin's achievements in Figure 5.3. Which three of these achievements do you think were the most important? Explain why you think they were important.

2 Study Extract B and Source P, which set out two different views of Lenin. Write your own obituary of Lenin. Think carefully about Lenin's achievements. Do you admire him for his loyalty and commitment to an idea? Think also about what these achievements cost. Do you despise Lenin for his cruel treatment of any opposition, or for the Red Terror? End your obituary with an assessment of what Lenin should be remembered for.

EXTRACT B

From an **obituary** of Lenin in a British newspaper, published on 23 January 1924.

The death of Lenin, the arch-traitor and conspirator, who was the chief agent in reducing Soviet Union to the pitiful condition in which she is today, it at last announced from Moscow. [Lenin was a] monster whose ruthless fanaticism was responsible for the deaths by direct means of over one million Russians, and indirectly, through need and starvation, for many millions more… The one excuse [for] his crimes is that he probably was sincere in the fanatical political creed [beliefs] he had adopted. But in the manner of its application in Russia there is no excuse…

SOURCE P

From a speech by Joseph Stalin about the death of Lenin, published on 30 January 1924.

Ours is the only country where the oppressed and downtrodden labouring masses have succeeded in throwing off the rule of the landlords and capitalists and replacing it by the rule of the workers and peasants. You know, comrades, and the whole world now admits it, that this gigantic struggle was led by Comrade Lenin and his Party… That explains why Lenin's name has become the name most beloved of the labouring and exploited masses.

RECAP

RECALL QUESTIONS

1 When was War Communism introduced and when did it end?
2 Is it true or false that during War Communism, half of Moscow's population left the city?
3 Which heroes of the Soviet Union's revolutions turned against the Bolsheviks in February 1921?
4 What did the Bolsheviks call the more wealthy peasants, who were blamed for resisting food requisition?
5 When did the Civil War finish?
6 What do the letters NEP stand for?
7 When did Russia change its name to the Soviet Union?
8 From 1923, food prices started to drop because of high levels of production, while manufactured products were still in short supply and so had high prices. What name did Trotsky use to describe this economic problem?
9 The 1920s saw the appearance of a new social group made up of traders who were making profits by selling products that were hard to find in shops. What term was used to describe this group?
10 Lenin died in January 1924. How old was he when he died?

CHECKPOINT

STRENGTHEN

S1 Identify two reasons why the Bolsheviks introduced War Communism in 1918.
S2 Identify two effects of War Communism that were also reasons for the introduction of the NEP in 1921.
S3 As a class, produce a revision mind map for each of the five topics covered in *Russia and the Soviet Union, 1905–24*. Share the mind maps out so you all have one for each topic.

CHALLENGE

C1 'Trotsky was the leader of the Petrograd Soviet. Trotsky was a much more popular speaker than Lenin, and Trotsky led the Red Army to victory in the Civil War. Trotsky's achievements were greater than Lenin's.' Make an argument against this view, explaining why Lenin's achievements were better than Trotsky's.
C2 Write two paragraphs using information from this chapter: one should explain the economic successes of the NEP and the second should explain the economic and social problems caused by the NEP.
C3 Do you think Lenin was right to pay foreign experts more than local workers for working in Russian industry?

SUMMARY

- Lenin introduced War Communism.
- War Communism gave the Bolsheviks greater control of the economy.
- War Communism was very unpopular with the peasants.
- Food shortages led to the Kronstadt Mutiny.
- The Bolsheviks won the Civil War in 1921.
- War Communism was replaced by the New Economic Policy.
- Nepmen made good profits as a result of the NEP.
- Lenin suffered two strokes in 1922.
- Lenin died in 1924.

EXAM GUIDANCE: PART (B) QUESTIONS

Study Sources A and B.

SOURCE A

A Communist revolutionary remembers the impact of the New Economic Policy.

The New Economic Policy was, in the space of a few months, already giving marvellous results. From one week to the next, the misery of the famine was sinking away. Restaurants were opening again and, wonder of wonders, pastries which were actually edible were on sale at a rouble apiece. The public was beginning to recover its breath, and people were talking about the return of capitalism, which they saw as the same thing as prosperity. On the other hand, the confusion among the party members was staggering. 'For what did we fight, spill so much blood, agree to so many sacrifices?' asked the Civil War veterans bitterly.

SOURCE B

From a book written by a leading Bolshevik. He is describing the impact of the New Economic Policy.

In just a few years, the NEP restored to Soviet Union an aspect of prosperity. But to many of us this prosperity was sometimes distasteful… There was gambling, drunkenness and all the old filth of former times… Classes were reborn in front of our eyes… There was a growing gap between the prosperity of the few and the misery of the many.

A03

SKILLS ANALYSIS, ADAPTIVE LEARNING, CREATIVITY

Question to be answered: How far does Source B support the evidence of Source A about the impact of the New Economic Policy?

Explain your answer. (8 marks)

1 **Analysis Question 1: What is the question type testing?**
In this question, you have to demonstrate that you can comprehend, interpret and cross-refer sources. In this question, that means you can see similarities and differences between two sources in what they say about the New Economic Policy.

2 **Analysis Question 2: What do I have to do to answer the question well?**
You have to write about points and areas of agreement and difference between the two sources that you are given. Do not be tempted to tell the examiner what each source says. The examiner will already know that! Go straight for the agreements and differences. You might, for example, say, 'The main areas of agreement between the two sources are…' or 'The sources both agree that…' or 'The two sources differ about…'.

3 **Analysis Question 3: Are there any techniques I can use to make it very clear that I am doing what is needed to be successful?**
This is an 8-mark question, and you need to be sure you leave enough time to answer the part (c) question, which is worth 16 marks. So you need to get straight in to your answer. Divide it into three parts. In the first paragraph, identify areas and points of agreement; in the second paragraph, do the same but identify differences. Remember to quote from the source material to support what you are saying. Your final paragraph should explain the extent of the support or agreement between the sources – that is, how strongly they agree or disagree.

You must identify both agreement and difference. You will get up to 5 marks for doing this and for supporting what you have selected with material from the sources. (You can only receive a maximum of 4 marks if you do 'just one side'.) There are 3 additional marks for explaining the extent to which one source supports the other.

Answer

There is a great deal of agreement between the sources about the impact of the New Economic policy. They agree that it had a good effect on Russia. According to Source A the New Economic Policy was already giving marvellous results, the misery of the famine was sinking away and 'people were talking about the return of capitalism, which they saw as the same thing as prosperity'. So that's a good thing. According to Source B 'In just a few years, the NEP restored to Soviet Union an aspect of prosperity'. So that sounds like it was a good thing too.

What are the strengths of this answer?

■ *Well there aren't many! I suppose we could say that agreement has been found between the sources and support given. But that's all.*

What are the weaknesses?

■ *There is no understanding that, actually, Source B does not think the NEP was a good thing, and so differs from Source A (which also includes some criticisms of it).*

Put it right!

■ *Look at the guidance in Analysis Question 3. Then rewrite the answer to turn it from a poor response into a high-scoring one.*

Answer checklist

☐ Identifies similarities
☐ Identifies differences
☐ Provides information from the sources to support the statements
☐ Considers the extent of the support/disagreement – which is stronger?

GLOSSARY

abdicate to give up the position of being king or queen

advance (v) to move towards someone or something, especially in a slow and determined way, particularly in a battle

alliance an arrangement in which two or more countries, groups, etc. agree to work together to try to change or achieve something. Military alliances are when countries promise to support each other if they face a threat

ammunition bullets, shells (shell), etc. that are fired from guns

aristocracy the people in the highest social class, who traditionally have a lot of land, money, and power

assassinate to murder an important person

asylum protection given to someone by a government because they have escaped from fighting or political trouble in their own country

authoritarian strictly forcing people to obey a set of rules or laws, especially ones that are wrong or unfair

autocracy a system of government in which one person or group has unlimited power

campaign (v) to lead or take part in a series of actions intended to achieve a particular social or political result

capitalist someone or a country that supports capitalism, an economic and political system in which businesses belong mostly to private owners, not to the government

ceasefire an agreement to stop fighting for a period of time, especially so that a more permanent agreement can be made

censorship the practice or system of removing anything that is considered offensive, morally harmful, or politically dangerous

chairperson someone who is in charge of a meeting or directs the work of a committee or organisation

civil rights the rights that every person should have, such as the right to vote or to be treated fairly by the law, whatever their sex, race or religion

civil war a war in which opposing groups of people from the same country fight each other in order to gain political control

coal mine a place from which coal, a hard black mineral that can be burnt to produce heat, is dug out of the ground

commune most Russian peasants did not have their own land, the community owned the land and all the peasant families in the community shared it

compensation money paid to someone because they have suffered injury or loss, or because something they own has been damaged

conscript (v) to make someone join the army, navy, etc.

conservative (n) someone who does not like changes in politics, ideas or fashion

consolidate to strengthen the position of power or success that you have, so that it becomes more effective or continues for longer

convict (v) to prove or officially announce that someone is guilty of a crime after a trial in a law court

crackdown action that is taken to deal more strictly with crime, a problem, protests, etc.

demonstrator someone who takes part in an event at which a large group of people meet to protest or to support something in public

deputy someone who is directly below another person in rank, and who is officially in charge when that person is not there

discrimination the practice of treating one person or group differently from another in an unfair way

empire a group of countries that are all controlled by one ruler or government

ethnic minority a group of people of a different race from the main group in a country

execute to kill someone, especially legally as a punishment

executive committee a committee at the head of a political party

exile (n) someone who has been forced to live in another country, especially for political reasons

exile (v) to force someone to leave their country, especially for political reasons

famine a situation in which a large number of people have little or no food for a long time and many people die

fleet a group of ships, or all the ships in a navy

follower someone who believes in a particular system of ideas, or who supports a leader who teaches these ideas

front the area where fighting happens in a war

general strike when workers in most or all key industries stop work as a protest

gentry people who belong to a high social class

grain the seeds of crops such as corn, wheat or rice that are gathered for use as food, or these crops themselves

heir to the throne the person who will become king or queen

imperialist a political system in which one country rules a lot of other countries

impose if someone in authority imposes a rule, punishment, tax, etc., they force people to accept it

industrialise if a country or area industrialises or is industrialised, it develops a lot of industry for the first time

inequality an unfair situation, in which some groups in society have more money, opportunities, power, etc. than others

interpretation the way in which someone explains or understands an event, information, someone's actions, etc.

Jew someone whose religion is Judaism, or who is a member of a group whose traditional religion is Judaism

labour work, especially physical work

left-wing a person or group that supports the political aims of groups such as the socialists and communists

legislation a law or set of laws

manifesto a written statement by a political party, saying what they believe in and what they intend to do

march (n) an organised event in which many people walk together to express their ideas or protest about something

massacre when a lot of people are killed violently, especially people who cannot defend themselves

middle class those belonging in the social class that includes people who are educated and work in professional jobs

middle ground ideas that are not extreme, and that people who oppose each other can agree about

migration when large numbers of people go to live in another area or country, especially in order to find work

monarchist someone who supports the idea that their country should be ruled by a king or queen

mystic involving religious, spiritual or magical powers that people cannot understand

nationalisation the act of bringing a company or industry under the control of a government

nationalist a nationalist organisation, party, etc., wants to gain or keep political independence for their country and people

naval relating to the navy or used by the navy

negotiate to discuss something in order to reach an agreement, especially in business or politics

negotiation official discussions between the representatives of opposing groups who are trying to reach an agreement, especially in business or politics

opposition strong disagreement with, or protest against, something such as a plan, law or system

overthrow to remove a leader or government from power, especially by force

peasant a poor farmer who owns or rents a small amount of land, either in past times or in poor countries

power vacuum a condition that exists when someone has lost control of something and no one has replaced them

propaganda information which is false or which emphasises just one part of a situation, used by a government or political group to make people agree with them

protester someone who takes part in a public activity such as a demonstration in order to show their opposition to something

province one of the large areas into which some countries are divided, and which usually has its own local government

ration (v) to control the supply of something because there is not enough

rebellion an organised attempt to change the government or leader of a country, using violence

redistribute to give something to each member of a group so that it is divided up in a different way from before

reform a change or changes made to a system or organisation in order to improve it

regime a government, especially one that was not elected fairly or that you disapprove of for some other reason

republic a country governed by elected representatives of the people, and led by a president, not a king or queen

resistance fighting against someone who is attacking you

retreat (n) a movement away from the enemy after a defeat in battle

revolt (n) strong and often violent action by a lot of people against their ruler or government

revolutionary someone who joins in or supports a political or social revolution

rig (v) dishonestly to arrange the result of an election or competition before it happens

right-wing supporting the ideas and beliefs of capitalism

riot a situation in which a large crowd of people are behaving in a violent and uncontrolled way, especially when they are protesting about something

rouble the standard unit of money in Russia

ruthless determined and firm when making unpleasant decisions

serfs peasants who lived and worked on land that they did not own and who had to obey the owner of the land

slogan a short phrase that is easy to remember and is used in advertisements, or by politicians, organisations, etc.

surrender to give up something or someone, especially because you are forced to

tabloid a newspaper that has small pages, a lot of photographs, and stories mainly about famous people, etc. rather than serious news

tactic a method that you use to achieve something

takeover an act of getting control of a country or political organisation, using force

telegraph an old-fashioned method of sending messages using radio or electrical signals

tonne a unit for measuring weight, equal to 1000 kilograms

traitor someone who is not loyal to their country, friends or beliefs

trigger (n) the thing that quickly causes something to happen

troop a group of soldiers, especially on horses or in tanks

tsar a male ruler of Russia until 1917

tsarist adjective describing a system of government controlled by a tsar

ultra-conservative someone who dislikes changes or new ideas to an extreme, especially in politics

unrest a political situation in which people protest or behave violently

upper class the group of people who belong to the highest social class

uprising an attempt by a group of people to change the government, laws, etc. in an area or country

voluntary organisation an organisation that is organised or supported by people who give their money, services, etc. because they want to and who do not intend to make a profit

whip (n) a long thin piece of rope or leather with a handle, that you hit animals with to make them move or that you hit someone with to punish them

withdraw if an army withdraws, or if it is withdrawn, it leaves a place

workaholic someone who chooses to work a lot, so that they do not have time to do anything else

working class the group of people in society who traditionally do physical work and do not have much money or power

INDEX